KARELIA

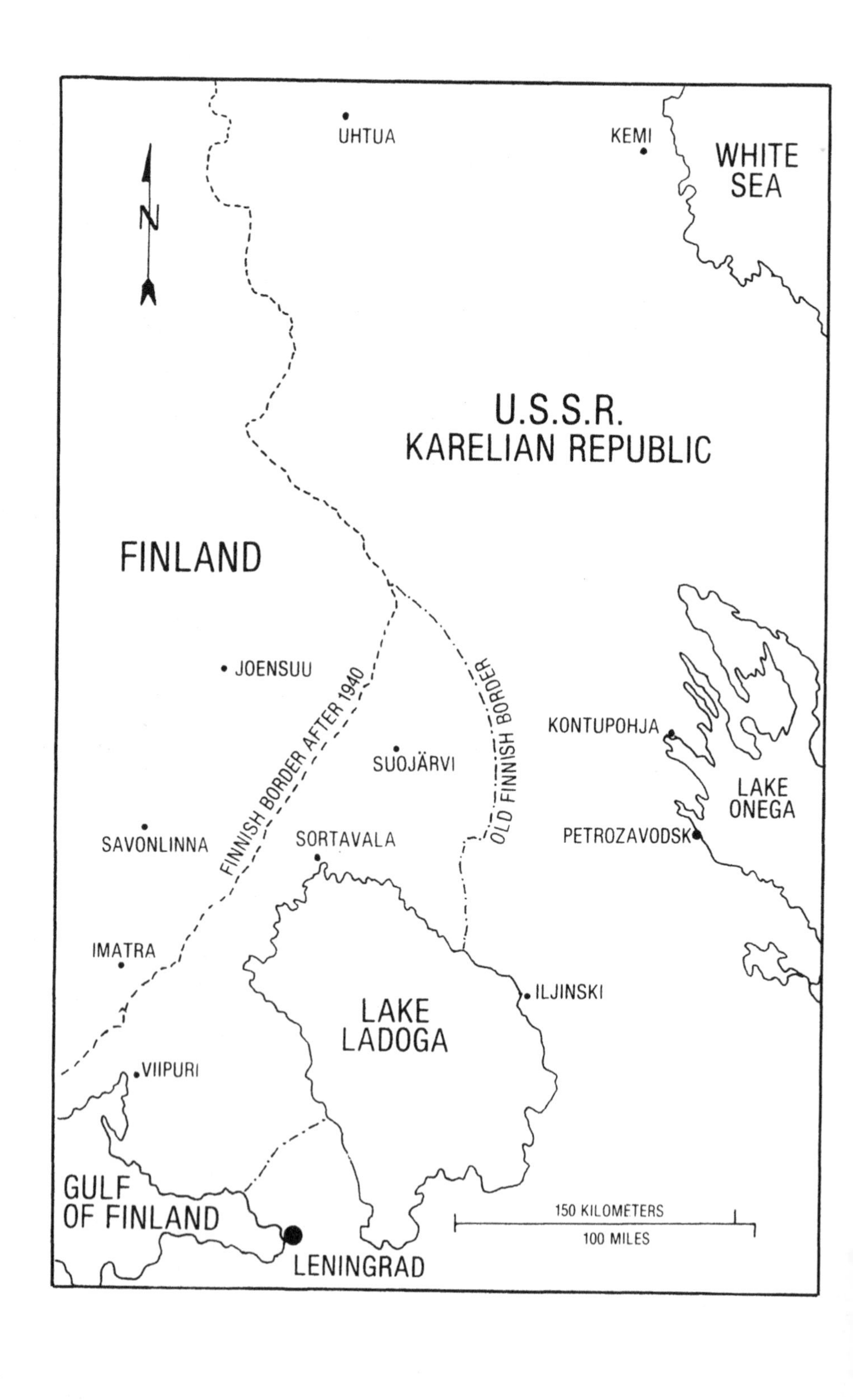
UHTUA
KEMI
WHITE SEA
N
U.S.S.R.
KARELIAN REPUBLIC
FINLAND
JOENSUU
FINNISH BORDER AFTER 1940
OLD FINNISH BORDER
KONTUPOHJA
SUOJÄRVI
LAKE ONEGA
PETROZAVODSK
SAVONLINNA
SORTAVALA
IMATRA
ILJINSKI
LAKE LADOGA
VIIPURI
GULF OF FINLAND
150 KILOMETERS
100 MILES
LENINGRAD

Karelia

A Finnish-American Couple in Stalin's Russia

Lawrence and Sylvia Hokkanen
with Anita Middleton

Library of Congress Cataloging-in-Publication Data

Hokkanen, Lawrence, 1909-
Karelia : A Finnish-American couple in Stalin's Russia / Lawrence and Sylvia Hokkanen with Anita Middleton.
160 p. 23 cm.
Includes bibliographical references.

1. Karel 'skaia A.S.S.R. (R.S.F.S.R.) — History. 2. Hokkanen, Lawrence, 1909- . 3. Hokkanen, Sylvia, 1913- . 4. Finnish-Americans — Russian S.F.S.R. — Karel 'skaia A.S.S.R. — Biography. 5. Soviet Union — History — 1925-1953. I. Hokkanen, Sylvia, 1913- . II. Middleton, Anita, 1942 . III. Title
DK511.K18H65 1991 91-32977
947'.25—dc20 CIP

Pen and Ink Drawings: Anita Middleton

Design: Corinne A. Dwyer

Foreword

This story has not been easy to write. The events took place almost sixty years ago, and much of what happened then has faded from memory—some was deliberately blocked out—and can no longer be retrieved. Recollection has been emotionally draining. Tears come easily, for what has not faded with the years, what still remains to haunt and torture us, is the fear—the stark panic of the times—the times of the Stalinist purges through which we lived. The memory of relatives and friends disappearing into the night has stayed with us through all these years.

Occasionally since that time, our daughter, Anita, and her husband, Len, would remind us that we ought to write the story of our life in Russia, but we did nothing. It was too painful to think about all that we and our friends had been through. Then too, we doubted that anyone would be interested. Finally we decided to try to recall as much as we could. Anita and Len, and even our grandchildren, have been very helpful. If it weren't for Anita, the story would even now remain unwritten; she has done a tremendous job of editing and arranging and typing—in addition to breathing down our necks. We especially appreciate the scholarly work done by Alexis Pogorelskin in providing an historical perspective to our story. Help has also come from several friends who have taken the time to read the story and have graciously submitted many helpful suggestions. We thank each one of them: particularly Flora Laun; also Hal Seppala, Bill and Nancy Saunders.

Now our story is complete, and we hope that you will find it interesting and thought-provoking.

Lawrence & Sylvia Hokkanen
Sugar Island, Michigan
September 1991

Lawrence and Sylvia Hokkanen in 1985. (Photo credit: Vivi Wiitala.)

Contents

Historical Preface

The memoir before you, while engaging in its own right, contributes to the understanding of a phenomenon of no small importance to both American social history and the history of the Soviet Union. That phenomenon is the "Karelian Fever" of the 1930s, when North American Finns, largely from the Upper Midwest and Canada, were lured to settle in Soviet Karelia to contribute to the building of communism. This subject, despite its significance, has received far too little scholarly attention and is little known, at least in this country, outside Finnish communities. For that reason alone, the labor that Lauri and Sylvi have performed, painful for them, deserves to be known.

As a professional historian I am not supposed to intrude into what I write, but in this instance the temptation is too great. Although possessing a doctorate in Russian history from Yale and having conducted research in numerous Soviet and European archives, I had never encountered a reference to Karelian Fever until coming to Duluth to teach at the University of Minnesota. I was stunned to discover neighbors and acquaintances who have relatives in the Soviet Union or who knew of those who had gone there and returned in the 1930s. Untapped sources of information about Stalin's Russia resided at my very doorstep.

I have twice been to Petrozavodsk and conducted research on Karelian Fever. The questions that formed in my mind were those of a Russian historian. Who decided to recruit American Finns to the Soviet Union and for what reason? Why Finns in particular? And finally, the question that seemed most important of all and yet whose answer might be most elusive: what impact would those foreigners have had on a closed society whose inhabitants had virtually no direct contact with the West?

After reading Lauri and Sylvi's story, I met with them, and our conversation provided an added dimension to their memoir. Lauri emphasized how distinctive were the Americans from the Soviets. Sylvi recounted that as she began to write each chapter she cried out of guilt over surviving what had destroyed so many others. A wonderfully cultured and informed person, she said she reads to understand the why of things. Their statements returned me to the questions that had already formed in my own mind. I will now attempt to address the why of Karelian Fever in my introduction to Sylvi and Lauri's memoir.

To understand Karelian Fever, one must begin with Edvard Gylling. Before becoming a Soviet citizen Gylling, as a Finn, had been a citizen of the Tsarist Empire. Russia had conquered the Grand Duchy of Finland from Sweden in 1809. The Finns retained a measure of administrative autonomy and appeared to prosper quietly under Russian control.

The apparent contentment of the Grand Duchy in fact hid a bitterly divisive issue that pitted the dominant Swedish minority against an exploited peasantry whose language was Finnish. Starting in the 1840s, a small group of Swedish intellectuals, calling themselves Fennomen, took up the cause of Finnish language and culture in opposition to their upper class brethren. Gylling joined the Fennomen early in his career but with the emergence of a Marxist party in the late 1890s he, along with "an important sector of Finnish-speaking intellectuals" abandoned the moderate Fennomen approach and joined the Marxist Social Democrats.[1]

As someone of uncommon abilities and a born politician, he played an important role in that particularly traumatic period of Finnish history, 1917-1918. Finland no sooner proclaimed its independence from Russia in December 1917, than the new nation was plunged into civil war. The landless Finnish peasantry and their Red Guards confronted the White forces representing the Swedish establishment. Gylling served as Minister of Finance in the revolutionary government that represented the cause of Finnish peasants and workers.[2]

By the spring of 1918 the Finnish radicals were clearly nearing defeat at the hands of Mannerheim and his troops. The new state of Soviet Russia offered Finnish Communists sanctuary there rather than see them massacred by Mannerheim's forces. Many, though not all, of the radicals were Communists. Gylling at that critical moment proposed to the Soviets that the Finns should settle in a seemingly obscure place of refuge, Soviet Karelia.[3] Gylling had several reasons for that suggestion. He wanted to develop the economic potential of a previously neglected region; he also saw Karelia as the base of a future Scandinavian Soviet Republic.[4] Gylling hoped that revolution would spread from Karelia to Finland and from there to the rest of Scandinavia. By monopolizing the forest wealth of Northern Europe, the Scandinavian Republic could subsidize revolution elsewhere and exert leverage on capitalist countries.[5] There is some confusion in the sources, but it seems that Lenin's government did not at first support Gylling's scheme, or at least its starting point, namely investment in the development of Soviet Karelia. Disappointed, Gylling, though a Communist, went into exile in Sweden rather than the Soviet Union. There he might have remained had not Finland and Soviet Russia begun an armed struggle for control of Karelia that raged well into 1919.[6] Finland agreed to negotiate that dispute and other outstanding issues at a conference to be convened in Dorpat, Estonia, in the fall of 1920. Lenin was determined to commence negotiations with the issue of Karelia already settled.

Gylling's previously eccentric interest in Karelia now became of prime importance. Lenin sent for him to come to Moscow and discuss the possibility of forming "an autonomous Karelian state in the Russian Socialist Republic."[7] Gylling could not help but heed Lenin's call because he was to be the "chief organizer" of the new state.[8] He placed certain conditions, however, on his cooperation. Those conditions grew out of his experience in the politico-linguistic conflicts of pre-war Finland. They were also supposed to forge Karelia as the starting point for the future Scandinavian Republic. That Lenin agreed to Gylling's conditions was a measure of his anxiety so close to negotiations with the Finns over the status of Karelia. He also recognized the merit of Gylling's argument that a stable, prosperous Karelia on the Finnish border held potential for the revolutionary cause throughout Northern Europe. No Karelian possessed the organizational abilities of Gylling. Lenin had to rely on him.

Gylling insisted that the region in population and language be Karelo-Finnish. Neither the Russian language nor a Russian population were to be allowed to dilute the ethnic homogeneity of the new state. Finally, at least a quarter of the profits from exploiting Karelian forests were to remain in Karelia.[9]

For Gylling the ethnic question was critical. As Kustaa Rovio, the first Secretary of the Karelian Communist Party and Gylling's closest associate observed, "If Russian *had* been made the language for the Karelians, the formation of an autonomous republic would have been nonsensical."[10] Gylling moved quickly to make Finnish the primary language of Karelia. He convinced Lenin that Karelian, without a written language of its own, was simply a Finnish dialect.[11] Therefore, Finnish along with Russian should be the state language of Karelia. In the absence of significant Russian immigration to Karelia, Finnish would remain the dominant language. Gylling very nearly refused to allow Petrozavodsk (the obvious choice because of its size and location) to serve as the capital of the new Karelian Workers' Commune on the grounds that it was already too Russian.

As long as Lenin lived, Gylling had his support for the existence of Karelia as a Karelo-Finnish enclave that would ignite revolution in Scandinavia. With the failure of Lenin's health in 1922, a tug of war for ethnic, (i.e. political), control of Karelia ensued. Hopelessly outnumbered, Gylling was bound to lose and be swallowed by Karelia's "host state," the greater Russian Soviet Republic.

Language, at first, constituted his primary weapon. In the early 1920s the Karelian Congress of Soviets cut the budget for Russian schools and extended financing to expand the network of Finnish schools. By 1931 "all schools in Karelian areas were operating in Finnish."[12] But Gylling could not stem the tide of Russian migration. At his insistance certain population ratios for Karelia had been established when the Treaty of Dorpat was signed.[13] By 1923 those ratios were a farce. In that year the Karelian Workers' Commune acquired new status as the Karelian Autonomous Republic. At the same time its territory was expanded, and 65,000 new inhabitants, mainly Russian, were added to its population.[14] Through the 1920s as many as four to five thousand Russians moved annually to Karelia, and Gylling frequently expressed concern over that fact.[15]

The situation became critical at the time that the first Five-Year Plan was launched in 1928. The imposition of a massive program of industrialization would provide an excuse for more intense immigration to Karelia. Party Secretary Rovio complained that Karelia's industrial work force was already "almost exclusively Russian." A new wave of Russian workers would overwhelm the more backward, agrarian Karelians whose Finnish identity Gylling had carefully nurtured through his language policy.[16]

Gylling now saw the economic potential of Karelia in direct conflict with the policy of Finnish ethnic identity which he had fostered in Karelia and supported throughout his career. The first Five-Year Plan put the issue in stark terms: how to reconcile the industrialization of Karelia and the Karelo-Finnish character of the region.

Through the course of 1929 and 1930 Gylling, Rovio and others spoke of the necessity of creating a "national proletariat" in Karelia.[17] In March 1931 Gylling began to implement a means to that end. He ordered the establishment of an Immigration Bureau to recruit labor for Karelia from elsewhere in the Soviet Union but also, the innovative addition, to recruit it from Canada and the United States.[18] Gylling's novel, yet seemingly obvious, solution to his ongoing struggle with Moscow for ethnic control of Karelia by 1931 had launched the phenomenon known as Karelian Fever.

There is an uncanny parallel between Gylling's political solution to his dilemma of the early 1930s and the central legend of the Finnish national epic, *The Kalevala*. Elias Lönnrot compiled the work in the 1840s from songs and folk tales in northern Karelia. More than a work of folklore, *The Kalevala* established a Finnish literary tradition and became the bible of the Fennomen movement. Gylling, as a committed Fennomen in his youth, would have been steeped in *The Kalevala*. There, the hero Ilmarinen, renowned for his mechanical skill and inventiveness, forges in a place called North Farm a wondrous device or miraculous mill called the Sampo, which churns out untold wealth and creates leisure. The Finns of North America, latter day Ilmarinens, traveled to the land of Kalevala and forged the "Sampo" of modern industrialization.

The Finnish communists of North America had a long record of support for Karelia and were known for their radical politics. A vehicle for recruitment among them had existed almost since the Russian Revolution. Gylling's Immigration Bureau worked through an organization called the Soviet-Karelian Technical Aid, an outgrowth of an earlier Society for Technical Aid to Soviet Russia, which began operation in New York in 1919. Its Karelian office (Karjalan Toimisto), through the 1920s had channeled assistance, mostly financial, to Karelia.[19] In fact, the Finnish communities of North America had organized "festivals, balls, theatrical performances, rallies and drives the proceeds from which were sent to the Karelian commune."[20] A few workers were recruited, but their numbers were negligible by comparison to what was to occur in the early 1930s.

Most sources maintain that as many as 10,000 people left North America for Karelia in the early 1930s, although one, probably erroneously, puts the figure at 5,000.[21] Kaarlo Tuomi, who went as a young boy with his family to Karelia, describes the mood of those people: "Group after group, in about two to three week intervals, left the shores of America full of dreams and determination to find what they considered a new and better world."[22]

Tuomi also describes the recruitment process in the Finnish communities. Enthusiastic speakers who had visited the Soviet Union on tours subsidized by the Communist Party gave glowing accounts of the character of life there with its unparalleled opportunities. Such accounts stood in stark contrast to the uncertainties of Depression-ridden America. A speaker would end his spiel with a screening of the Soviet propaganda film "The Old and the New" to dispel any doubts that might remain.[23]

The experience of Lauri's mother is probably typical for a whole generation of Finnish immigrants in North America. She was a regular reader of the Finnish-American radical newspaper *Työmies* (Workingman) which painted a serene picture of equity and fairness in the Soviet Union. "In the *Työmies* it all sounded great."[24] Kaarlo Tuomi has explained that, on the pages of that newspaper, Finns were treated to a regular dose of items from the British communist newspaper *The Daily Worker*, which, in turn, received much of its material from *Pravda*.[25] In the early 1920s, moreover, *Työmies* was filled with articles by Finnish communists who had fled to the Soviet Union and used it to proselytize for their cause.[26] Linguistically isolated and knowing little if any English, many immigrants relied on *Työmies* for their information which, it is now clear, was hopelessly skewed and inaccurate.

Other less obvious factors existed to encourage North American Finns to immigrate to Karelia. The appeals were made directly to them. The ads in *Työmies* in the early 1930s informed applicants that they must submit to Karelian Technical Aid "a recommendation from a Finnish Workers' Association or from two association officials."[27] There were certainly other immigrant groups known for skills in forestry and construction to which Gylling and Rovio could have appealed. They did not. It was important that they recruit not only a competent work force (which the Finns certainly were) but also an ethnically Finnish and Finnish-speaking one as well.

Finns responded to a cause that was clearly their own. Simply put, recruitment to Karelia engendered Finnish national pride. The issue of pride was an important one for Finnish immigrants who felt isolated and even scorned. In Sinclair Lewis' novel *Cass Timberlane*, set in the Minnesota of the 1930s, he refers to a pecking order among Scandinavian immigrants. The Finns were at the bottom of it. This unfortunate situation had grown out of the intense animosities between Finnish and Swedish speakers in Finland. The language conflict, in fact, dominated Finnish politics from the 1860s onward. Encouraged by the extreme Swedish nationalist A. O. Freudenthal, Swedish militants had "adopted the racist doctrines of the time to brand Finns as racially inferior."[28]

Such doctrines encouraged Finnish migration to America. Transported here, they discouraged Finnish assimilation in the new world. One appeal of Karelian recruitment, and hence its transformation into a "fever," lay in its endowing Finnish immigrants with significance and a special purpose. Some went to Karelia to find a self-esteem that had eluded them in America. Some went, like Lauri and Sylvi, because they were intelligent and hard working. They saw opportunity elsewhere at a time when the American dream seemed further than ever from realization. Some went to fulfill a commitment to the ideal of Communism. Some went to escape a business failure or the grief of a death in the family. Karelian Fever gave one particular ethnic group in America a unique opportunity to undergo a total change in their lives in what was a decade of uprootings. As Woodie Guthrie's songs of wanderlust from the 1930s reveal, Americans, out of necessity, were on the move.

Gylling's very policy of recuiting North American Finns proved his undoing. To begin with, even 10,000 immigrant Finns did not suffice as a counterweight to Russian immigration into Karelia.[29] Even before such recruitment began. Moscow had deplored the "Finnicization" of Karelia, and the early 1930s saw increasingly adverse attention given to policies in Karelia which allegedly "fostered withdrawal into a national shell."[30]

By the spring of 1935 the leaders of the Leningrad party organization, which had jurisdiction over the Karelian party apparatus, were openly attacking "local nationalism" in Karelia.[31] The policy of recruiting North American Finns was clearly over. Sylvi mentions that already by 1934 the fever had begun to subside.[32] She and Lauri left with only eight others and there was no celebration at their departure from New York as had occurred with groups that left earlier. Gylling's policy was already in trouble.

In addition to the ethnic question, Stalin had other reasons for eliminating Gylling and his programs. In late 1933, only months before Lauri and Sylvi's departure, the Soviet Union had obtained long-coveted diplomatic recognition by the United States. Stalin wanted the Americans to join him in curbing Japanese expansion in the Pacific. Vigorous recruitment of American workers to a better life in Soviet Union could not help but antagonize his new-found ally. Gylling's efforts were undermining Stalin's diplomacy. Gylling himself constituted a phenomenon also anathema to Stalin: he was a popular figure who dominated the local administrative apparatus that he himself had created. Gylling had run Karelia since 1920. He would have to go. In the fall of 1935 both Rovio and Gylling were removed from their positions in Karelia.

With Gylling's departure and the discrediting of his policies, the North American Finns became isolated. They remained a minority within a minority as no new waves of immigrants arrived. The special INSNAB stores which had catered only to the newcomers were closed, and the kind of personal contact with Rovio and Gylling which Lauri and Sylvi describe was no longer possible with the new leadership.

What had begun to appear ominous in 1935 turned into a nightmare by 1937 and 1938. In 1937 Gylling and Rovio were executed. They were destroyed in a holocaust that victimized much of the command structure of the Soviet Union. In Karelia the victims were those communists who had fled Finland in 1918 and those North American Finns who had joined the communist party, that is, those who had administered the region.

The regime held back at first from touching those Finns who had never joined the communist party or who had not renewed their North American party membership in Karelia as was required. It was possible that Stalin regarded such people as genuine foreigners. He was courting Western aid against Hitler. Executing westerners could antagonize the very governments whose assistance he sought.

But in July 1938 the turn came for non-party members among the Finnish immigrants. Lauri's account of the "*suuri kauhu*" or "great terror" is chilling. The Finnish language was banned. Those events coincided with the initiation of Soviet pressure on Finland to cede it certain strategic territory. Soviet demands culminated in the Winter War with Finland in 1939. Stalin's regime could regard its Finnish minority as a potentially disloyal element in the event of war with Finland. In the summer of 1938 it had begun brutally to prepare for that eventuality. Only a few such as Lauri and Sylvi miraculously survived along with the younger generation of Finns that had barely reached adulthood by 1938.

By way of epilogue, I will turn to the question: did nothing good come of the high hopes and enthusiasm among Finns infected with Karelian Fever? An answer emerges from this memoir. Repeatedly one is struck with how distinctive were the North American Finns in Karelia. Almost inadvertently Lauri and Sylvi describe a competence, mechanical training, technical inventiveness, over-all quality of work, standard of cleanliness and generosity of spirit which set the foreigners apart. Soviets who would otherwise never see the West for themselves were exposed to Western standards and mores simply by living in Karelia starting in the 1930s.

One such individual was Yuri Andropov, later head of the secret police and party General Secretary. He ruled the Soviet Union along with Brezhnev from 1967 and then singly from 1982 to 1984. He mentored Gorbachev and advanced him as his successor. Observers have long wondered at Andropov's awareness of Western standards. He introduced computers to the KGB, made its agents study foreign languages, and encouraged Gorbachev's early travels abroad.

The solution to the Andropov puzzle overwhelmed me on my first visit to Petrozavodsk. I encountered survivors and descendents of the North American migration all over town. Some remembered Andropov. To honor him, a local museum devoted an exhibition to the period of his life spent in Karelia, from the late 1930s to the early 1950s. There was his foreign language dictionary. He had worked with those who, in the late 1930s, belonged to the younger generation of North American Finns. Too young to be party members, they had escaped the holocaust that destroyed their parents. They had exposed him to the West; and they were the source of his hitherto unexplained knowledge of English.

Finally, I will describe an evening in the summer of 1991 in the home of Sylvi and Lauri's daughter. The occasion was a party in honor of visiting dignitaries from Petrozavodsk. Sylvi and I sat in a corner while she told me how emotionally traumatic it was for her to remember her Karelian experiences. She cried quietly. I thought, if she and Lauri and others like them had not gone to Russia, Gorbachev might never have come to rule the Soviet Union or at least not have initiated the policies of openness and modernization his exposure to the West encouraged. Andropov had initiated Gorbachev to the West. Something positive had come of Karelian Fever after all.

Alexis Pogorelskin, Ph.D.
University of Minnesota
Duluth

Notes

1 Gylling had traded liberalism for radicalism. Nonetheless, he had been formed in a society where Finnish language and culture had had to fight for their right to exist against the dominant Swedish culture and the overlordship of Russia. Gylling never forgot those early experiences. Peter Kivisto, "Pre-Migration Factors Contibuting to the Development of Finnish-American Socialism," *Finnish Americana*, 1982-83, p. 26.

2 John H. Hodgson, *Communism in Finland: A History and Interpretation*, Princeton University Press, 1967, p. 147; Arvo Tuominen, *The Bells of the Kremlin*, University Press of New England (Hanover, New Hampshire), 1983, p. 282.

3 Ibid, Hodgson.

4 Z. Strogal'shchikova, "S uchetom proshlogo," recent Karelian newspaper unattributed; Tuominen, p. 45, 46.

5 Ibid.

6 Hodgson, p. 152.

7 Tuominen, p. 282.

8 Ibid.

9 Tuominen, p. 282.

10 Hodgson, p. 156.

11 Tuominen, p. 285-285.

12 Hodgson, 156-158.

13 Tuominen, p. 284.

14 Ibid.

15 In *Punainen Karjala*: 8 Oct. 1927; 28 July 1929; 31 March 1931; as cited in Hodgson, p. 161.

16 Ibid.

17 Hodgson, p. 161.

18 Ibid.

19 Auvo Kostiainen, "The Forging of Finnish-American Communism, 1917-1924," *Turun Yliopiston Julkaisuja*, Ser. B., Vol. 147, 1978, p. 164.

20 Ibid.

21 Piltti Heiskanen. Editor's note in *Bells of the Kremlin* by Arvo Tuominen.

22 Kaarlo Tuomi, "The Karelian Fever of the Early 1930s," *Finnish Americana*, Vol III (1980), p. 63.

23 Ibid, p. 62-63.
24 Text, p. 2.
25 Tuomi, p. 63.
26 Kostiainen, p. 160.
27 *Työmies*, undated.
28 Kivisto, p. 24.
29 Hodgson, p. 164.
30 Ibid, p. 165.
31 Ibid, p. 167.
32 Text, p. 14.

References

Heiskanen, Piltti. Editor's note in *Bells of the Kremlin* by Arvo Tuominen.

Hodgson, John H. *Communism in Finland: A History and Interpretation.* Princeton University Press, 1967.

Kivisto, Peter. "Pre-Migration Factors Contributing to the Development of Finnish-American Socialism." *Finnish Americana* 1982-83.

Kostiainen, Auvo. "The Forging of Finnish-American Communism 1917-24." *Turun Yliopiston Julkaisuja* Ser. B., Vol. 147, 1978.

Rovio, Kustaa. "*Kielikysymys Neuvosto-Karjalan Kansallisuus-politiikassa.*" *Kommunisti* No. 8 (80) August 1931, p. 385, as quoted in Hodgson, p. 156.

Strogal'shchikova, Z. "S *uchetom proshlogo.*" Recent Karelian newspaper unattributed.

Tuomi, Kaarlo. "The Karelian Fever of the Early 1930s." *Finnish Americana.* Vol. III (1980).

Tuominen, Arvo. *The Bells of the Kremlin.* University Press of New England. Hanover, N.H., 1983.

Sylvi and Lauri Hokkanen.

It Couldn't Have Happened

L: "That couldn't have happened," my mother said, and she turned away. A quick-tempered, strong-willed little woman, she made it very clear that she did not want to hear any more.

I had been trying to tell her what our lives had been like in the Soviet Union where my wife, Sylvi, and I had spent the last seven years. We had just returned to the United States, that spring of 1941, with almost nothing but the clothes on our backs and feeling lucky to have gotten out safely. I wanted to tell my mother what we had gone through in Russia, and I tried, but what she said was, "That couldn't have happened." "Couldn't have," when I had just told her it did. Why didn't she believe me? What reason could she have had to doubt her own son's story about things that he had seen and heard and actually experienced?

Lauri Hokkanen (L)

I think the problem was that what happened to us, and to so many others in Soviet Karelia, went against the political beliefs that she had held very strongly for most of her life. Her view of the world had been shaped by the Finnish-American radical newspaper, *Työmies* (*The Worker*), that she read every week. She was a kind-hearted woman, and she really believed that in the communist "workers' paradise" every man would have a chance to make a good life for himself. That was the plan: "From each according to his ability; to each according to his need." There wouldn't be a ruling class that had all the money and a working class that had a hard time finding jobs to pay enough to feed a family. Everyone would be a worker, and everyone would share alike.

This "workers' paradise," my mother also knew from her newspaper, was being created and lived out in the Soviet Union, a glorious country where no one went hungry and where the communist party, a group of loyal, dedicated and unpaid workers with the highest of ideals, saw to it that everything was done right. In *Työmies* it all sounded great.

Now here we were, just returned from that wonderful place, scared half to death and telling her about arrests, disappearances, beatings, escapes. The dream that she had believed in and worked for ever since she was a girl was sounding like a nightmare.

Sylvi was angry with mother for refusing to believe me, but I felt that she really was not *able* to believe it. Many things that happened over there had been hard for *us* to believe, even while they were happening to us! So many innocent people arrested—people we knew, good friends—and never heard from again. It didn't make any sense. We gave up trying to tell my mother about it. She was very sick with arthritis at that time, so we felt it best to treat her the way we always had and not aggravate her.

Mother wasn't the only one who didn't want to hear what we had to say about Russia. There were others back home in Michigan who had their own ideas about what was going on in the Soviet Union and didn't want them disturbed. There was one man from Sault Ste. Marie, for instance, who had been to Karelia himself for a very short time and returned to the states because he could not live on the Soviet diet. He came to see us after we returned and told us right out that no one had been arrested in the Soviet Union who was not guilty. Of course he didn't know anything about it; he had returned before the purges. But there was no changing his mind.

There were also people who were suspicious of us. Why were we allowed to come back when others couldn't? Some people thought they had it all figured out. Behind our backs, they said we had to be spies for the Soviet Union or we never would have gotten permission to return. I suppose it made a good story. And we certainly couldn't explain, and can't to this day, why we were among the very few who were allowed to come back from Soviet Karelia.

So, after we returned to the United States, we didn't talk much about the experiences we had had. We never knew whether other people wanted to hear our story, and, many times, other people weren't sure whether we would want to talk about it and hesitated to ask. If someone who knew where we had been asked a question, we would answer, but we never told any new friends or acquaintances where we had lived between 1934 and 1941. We just never mentioned it. We didn't even tell our daughter, born the year after we returned, the whole story. We had a few items, just trinkets really, from Russia and Japan. When she asked how we had gotten these things, we told her we had been around the world on our honeymoon. It was stretching the truth a little—seven years is a long honeymoon!

In the fifties, when Senator Joe McCarthy was hunting down communists and communist sympathizers and anyone who had ever had anything to do with communists, some FBI agents asked some of our neighbors in Detroit about us. Our good friend Mary, next door, came and told us about it. It scared us. It was too much like being back in Russia. But nothing ever happened to us. We had never been party members anyway.

In 1984, fifty years after we left for the Soviet Union, we decided to tell our story. We decided, before Mikhail Gorbachev had even been elected General Secretary, that it was time for our own "glasnost." Stalin's crimes were pretty well known by then, and many of the families of those who had been arrested had received word that their relatives had been cleared of any crime—posthumously.

Sylvi and I have spent many hours trying to remember all the things that happened to us so many years ago when we set off on what we thought was going to be an exciting adventure. There are probably still some people who will not want to believe this story. We don't blame them. It is hard to believe that men can do the things that we have seen. It is also hard to understand how a system that was intended to benefit the working man could turn out so differently. But we have tried to be scrupulously honest and tell everything just as we remember it.

To Build a Workers' Paradise

S: Lauri and I grew up on Sugar Island which is located in the St. Mary's River below Sault Ste. Marie, Michigan. The island was originally inhabited by Indians; then French and Irish moved in. In the early nineteen hundreds a Finnish land agent persuaded many Finns from Michigan's Upper Peninsula and Canadian mining communities to move to Sugar Island to try their hand at farming. Our parents were among them.

Sylvi Hokkanen (S)

These first generation American-Finns were literate and culture-conscious people. Although most of them spoke only Finnish, they kept up with world events by means of Finnish language newspapers. Their children, including Lauri and me, spoke only Finnish when they entered school but learned English very quickly. A few discarded their mother tongue in embarrassment. In a reverse situation, when Lauri entered kindergarten, all except two of the children were Finnish. The teacher was English, and classes were conducted in English, but at recess, of course, the Finnish language held sway. By the end of the year, all of the children spoke Finnish, including the two non-Finns, who then retained it for the rest of their lives.

Many of the Finns who settled on Sugar Island were politically oriented towards the left and joined the workers' movements: first the Socialists, and later the Communist Party. My father, Frank Kuusisto, donated a corner of his farm land for the construction of a hall where political meetings and social events could be held. There were dances, box socials, sporting events and plays—some comedies and some with a political message, always leftist. Even those Finns who were not interested in politics joined in all the other activities for they constituted the social life at the time. And, in those pre-babysitter days, when the parents went out, the children did too. It was also our social life. We learned to dance and do athletics soon after learning to walk. We had opportunities to perform in plays, and many Finns became very able actors and actresses. Lauri and I appeared in a few plays at our Sugar Island Hall, though neither of us really got into acting.

The depth of commitment to the workers' movement seems to have varied from generation to generation. As far as our families were concerned, I am not sure how our grandparents in Finland felt. They were poor, hard-working people with deep religious faith. They probably bore their hardships quietly, believing that the hereafter would bring a better life for them. But our parents, both Lauri's and mine, had begun to look at conditions from a workers' viewpoint. They saw the unjust way the state church of Finland treated the poor. The tithing system was in full force; the church had to have its full share regardless of whether or not there was anything left for the family. The landowner also had to have his share, leaving the poor tenant farmer with very little on which to survive. Our parents and many others came to America hoping for a better, easier life away from the oppression of state church and landed gentry. But here, too, they saw oppression and exploitation of the worker, especially the immigrant worker who, partly because of the language barrier, was unable to fight for his rights. And so they joined the American socialist movement, which at that time was quite strong.*

---

*It is estimated that twenty-five to forty percent of the Finnish immigrant population participated in radical political groups. (Kivisto 16).

After the revolution in Russia there came a turning point in the socialist movement: those who felt that revolution was the best solution to the problems of the working class turned to communism; those who thought that improvements should come through peaceful means followed socialist tactics. This division caused much bitterness among the American Finns. Our parents, at this point, joined the communists. They believed that the Soviet Union had done the right thing in revolting, and they were willing to follow Russia's lead. They were sure the Soviet Union would truly become a workers' paradise.

Some of the Finns of our generation, the second generation, became interested in politics and carried on the beliefs of our elders. My oldest brother, for one, became a communist party youth organizer, but he died of tuberculosis at the age of twenty-one, so I cannot say how deeply committed he would have been when older. Some few from Sugar Island rose in the ranks of the communist party; others joined the union movement.

But many of us who left home at an early age to work (like Lauri) or to go to school (as I did) grew away from the political activism of our parents. We hadn't, as yet, fully understood what they were striving for, or what the true meaning of communism was. The slogans were great, the workers' anthem was inspiring, but there were so many other things that occupied our minds. Lauri was working on the lake freighters, in lumber camps and sawmills. I finished my schooling and began to teach in the fall of 1931, and it was that same fall that Lauri and I started "going together."

Lauri was a very handsome, personable young man, clearly the type who could sweep a young woman off her feet. He was ambitious, eager to work at most any kind of job to make a good living. I was irresistibly drawn to him, although he was considered by some of the older generation to be a bit on the wild side. An elderly lady, a dear and close friend of ours, even went so far as to warn me against marrying "that wild one"—a warning that (fortunately for me) I decided to ignore. My father approved of Lauri whole-heartedly. And so, in December of 1932, the day after Christmas, we were married.

Our decision to go to the Soviet Union was made not long after our marriage. Since the 1920s there had been a great need in Soviet Karelia for technical aid and for skilled lumber workers with tools and machines. They were needed to harvest the vast forests of Karelia for export in exchange for *valuutta* (foreign currency) which was sorely needed by the Soviet government for trading with other countries. The Finnish workers' organizations in Canada and the United States, in cooperation with Moscow, had begun to recruit workers with this in mind. Then in 1931 the Soviet government set up the Karelian Technical Aid organization to manage the recruitment process.

Headquartered in the Harlem area of New York City, Karelian Technical Aid employed several recruiters who traveled around to Finnish communities in the United States and Canada making speeches about the wonderful opportunities for workers in Soviet Karelia. Those who signed up were organized into groups, and Karelian Technical Aid arranged for their transportation to Russia from New York. The recruiters were quite successful. It has been estimated that as many as ten thousand Finns from the United States and Canada emigrated to Karelia in the thirties. The passion to go and build a workers' paradise became so strong and so prevalent that it was known as "Karelian Fever."

The fact that the United States was in the grip of the Great Depression naturally made the communist experiment in Russia look more attractive. We had read in the paper about the stock market collapse (known as "Black Friday"), on October 28, 1929, and we heard about people who had committed suicide after losing all their money. This made us wonder what the future would hold for us on Sugar Island. At the same time, we read in the *Työmies* about the many job opportunities and freedom from exploitation in the Soviet Union.

Some of our relatives answered the recruiters' call early in the thirties. Lauri's cousin Lily, her husband Dave Metsälä and their two children, Viola and Hugo, from Ontonagon, Michigan, went to Karelia before we did. Dave went first and, we learned later, did not like what he found. He wrote to Lily not to come, and that he would return as soon as he could. But she had progressed too far with her preparations to leave—the house was sold, the farewell parties were over—and so she followed him anyway. Among my relatives, my mother's brother Frank Pihlava went with his wife and their son, Arvo. An older girl, Eva, had elected to stay in the States.

Few people went from Sugar Island. There was a family named Soini, whom we never heard of again, and three single fellows: John Boman, Victor Viiki and our friend, Albin Heino. Heino was the only one we had heard from; he had written, urging us to come too. There would be work for Lauri, he said, and for me a chance to continue my schooling and teaching. I had taught school for two years, from the fall of 1931 to the summer of 1933, but at that time people looked askance at married women who held jobs that could have gone to single people, and so I had given it up.

It was difficult, though. Teaching had been my dream since I was a little girl. I had completed the eight grades in a Sugar Island school, then high school in Sault Ste. Marie, and I had even had two years of college with great financial sacrifice on the part of my father and brothers.* (My mother had died when I was thirteen.) So the two years I was able to teach on Sugar Island were indeed a dream come true. I taught in the same one-room school I had attended as a child, and my pupils were Finnish and Indian children of neighboring families. I enjoyed it very much and giving it up was not easy, but I did have hopes of continuing my education in the Soviet Union—if indeed we did go there.

Although Lauri was doing well at that time running the sawmill that he had purchased from Heino, he was worried about the future. Those of us living in the country had not been hit as hard by the Depression as city dwellers. We had our vegetables, our milk, fish and venison. But even for us, money was hard to come by, and we would resort to bartering. Lauri often had to take lumber for pay when sawing logs for neighbors. Then he would try to sell the lumber for cash in order to buy fuel. White pine was twenty-five dollars for one-thousand board feet delivered—certainly a bargain if you had the cash. At the suggestion of a neighbor, Lauri purchased a grain grinder which he set on a trailer so he could move it around. With it, he ground wheat, barley and oats for the neighboring farmers, and they would give him flour in return. So we were getting along all right, but the future did not look promising in the United States at that time. Of course we didn't expect to find wealth and material comforts in the Soviet Union, but we did feel that there would be an opportunity to work for a better life with a good chance of success.

We decided to apply. Immigrants to Soviet Karelia had to be cleared by the Karelian Technical Aid organization and also by the American Communist Party. Although the party was, of course, in favor of helping Karelia and all of Russia improve their economic status, it did not want to lose its best political workers and comrades in the United States. So the preferred recruits were middle-aged to elderly people who spoke only Finnish and would therefore be less able to help with the class struggle here. Although we were young and spoke English, we were not party members and were more or less apolitical. So the party probably felt that we could best serve their purposes in Karelia, especially with our

*In 1928, at the age of fifteen, Sylvia Kuusisto was the youngest person ever to graduate from the Sault high school.

lumbering and teaching skills. At any rate, we received permission to go.

Most of the immigrants took with them all they could afford of clothing, food and tools. Many used all their savings to buy whatever could be used in Karelia: cars, trucks, farm machinery. Some sold their homes and farms, getting very low prices for them because of the Depression. They were urged to make donations, if they could, to the "machine fund" of either money or tools and machines, and many did.

We had no savings to donate. In the spring of 1933, when I was still teaching, money was so scarce in the Sault that the banks issued scrip instead of money. This was fine as long as we were using it locally, but when we decided to go to Karelia we had to have cash for our fares. So we hoarded all the coins we got in change, and Lauri was fortunate enough to find a buyer for the sawmill who had real cash, a man on Drummond Island who had kept his money under his mattress.

In order to deliver the mill, Lauri hired a trucker friend to drive it across the ice. The ice was thick, but the mill was a heavy load; they kept the cab doors open all the way, ready to jump out if the ice gave way. The St. Mary's River ice was tricky due to the strong current and to springs in the river bottom. We knew of several cars and teams of horses that had broken through and been lost over the years, but it was the only way to get across to the mainland in winter, and folks often took chances. Fortunately, Lauri and his friend had no trouble. The mill was delivered, and we had the cash for our transportation to Russia.

Our preparations to leave were quite simple. Compared to others, we took little. We had no savings to spend. As for clothing, we just took what we had, feeling that we should make do with whatever was available in the Workers' Paradise. Surely we could manage where others did. We took one pound of A & P Bokar, our favorite brand of coffee at the time. Lauri took what tools he had; they were mostly for auto repair. We also had our friend Albin Heino's tools with us. He had left them behind and now wanted us to bring them. We did take one big piece of furniture, a Simmons hide-a-bed sofa. We knew furniture was scarce over there, and, a good bed being essential to one's physical well-being, we made this one exception. One of our pieces of luggage was unusual: an old wooden box the size of a large trunk that had been used by my father in the barn for storing oats. We emptied and cleaned it as best we could. Much later I wondered where my poor father stored his oats after we took his box to the ends of the earth.

Before we left, our friends gave us a going-away party. It was held at the Hall. We danced and enjoyed the usual cakes and coffee. A collection had been taken earlier, and at the party we were presented with a "going-away" gift: a genuine Hudson's Bay blanket. It was a wonderful gift. We took it with us and made good use of it.

On a sad day in May 1934, I bade good-bye to my father and brothers. This parting was most heartbreaking for me, for I had a very close relationship, especially with my father and my brother Andrew, who was only a year and a half younger than I. Brother Arvo was six years younger and did not feel as close. Although I had been away at school since I was eleven years old, this parting was different. I would be very far away . . . in another world, so to speak. As hard as this parting was for me, parting with my wonderful young husband would have been unbearable. My place was with him, and so I followed him gladly, though tearfully. As I said good-bye to my father and brothers, I wondered when, if ever, I would see them again. It was to be my last good-bye to Andrew and my father.

I have often wondered how our folks, my father and Lauri's mother and father, felt about our going to Karelia. As I recall, they neither urged us to go nor did they advise us against it. Stoic Finns that they were, they did not speak much of their feelings. My father must have felt his loss deeply; I was the only girl in the family, and we were very close. Furthermore, after years of struggling to help me get an education, he was now on the point of getting some return for his investment. I doubt that this was on his mind, but I myself have often regretted leaving him at this point. I wonder if perhaps our parents thought of our going as a gift from them to the Soviet Union; since they could not go, the next best thing was to send us instead. I may be wrong; I may be right.

The first leg of our journey took us as far as Detroit, where we spent a few days with our friends Paul and Ingrid Middleton. They were a Finnish couple; their name had been Muttilainen originally. Paul's sister Martha, her husband, Dave Nieminen, and their daughter, Ella, had gone to Karelia in 1931.

We continued by bus to New York City. There, too, we remained for a few days in a hotel near the Karelian Technical Aid headquarters in Harlem until the rest of our group arrived. Then, at last, we boarded the ship *Majestic*, headed for England.

Ours was a small group compared to those that had gone before us. By 1934 the "Karelian Fever," which had peaked during the first years of the decade, had died down. There were only about ten people in our group, and we held no political meetings, no programs, no flag waving or hurrahs as the earlier, larger groups had been in the habit of doing. These earlier groups were well organized with elected officials, entertainment committees, and rules of conduct. They held meetings and social events, and in this way kept up their spirits and their sense of camaraderie. Red flags were everywhere and were waved at farewells and also for greetings when stopping at foreign ports. Although we did none of these things, we were also a dedicated group and on the way to help as best we could in building a workers' land.

The ocean trip was most unpleasant for me since I suffered with seasickness much of the way. On our first morning, as we set out for a walk on deck, Lauri suddenly grabbed me and turned me around saying, "Don't look that way!" All around us, people were vomiting over the side of the ship. Soon, unfortunately, I was one of them, but Lauri never felt sick at all and enjoyed the meals all the way across. Later, on the North Sea, seasickness again hit me, to the point where I fainted dead away and thought I was dying.

Early in June we landed in Southampton, England, and continued from there by train to London, where we stayed for three or four days in modest accommodations arranged for us by Karelian Technical Aid. This short stay convinced me that I did not care for English cuisine; to me, it seemed heavy and indigestible. However, had my taste of English food followed our stay in Karelia, the verdict might have been different.

It had been said that more older people came back in short order because they could not cope with the realities of life in Karelia. Many of them had lived through a harsh childhood in Finland, had immigrated to the United States or Canada and, with hard work and many deprivations, had managed to attain a fairly good life. Now they had given this up and once again faced hard work and primitive conditions. Poor diet, especially the sour black bread so common in Russia, brought on health problems, and it was too much for many of them. But coming back did not necessarily mean that they disapproved of the concept of a workers' paradise, nor did they withdraw their support of the Soviet Union. Young people, on the other hand, were more often able to adapt to life in Russia. They were full of strength and vitality and imbued with the idea of a classless society, although perhaps not so class conscious as their elders. They took the hardships in stride, believing that everything would improve in time.

We were part of this latter group. We expected life in Karelia to be difficult, especially at first. But we were sure that with hard work and the support of so many comrades with the same vision, things would soon change for the better. We had a dream.

Bedbugs, Bricks and Big Trees

L: I had worked in lumber camps, on lake freighters and in saw mills ever since I had finished the eighth grade and had learned quite a bit about mechanics from running the mills and from repairing boats and automobiles. It was the kind of work I liked to do. After Heino left I became curious about the opportunities in Karelia. It sounded like everyone who went there was doing all right. Sylvi and I were both healthy and just wanted a chance to use our skills and make a living. We never ruled out the idea that we might want to come back to the United States some day.

I was also fascinated with the idea of seeing other countries and peoples. It was exciting to go overseas. My first taste of being a foreigner came in London when I went to buy some ink. The clerk had no problem understanding me but when she said, "That'll be tuppence," I had no idea what she meant.

"Tuppence . . . tuppence," she repeated.

By this time I felt really foolish and extended a handful of change from which she, laughing merrily, extracted two pennies. With a sheepish grin, I left in a hurry.

A few days later, we boarded the Russian ship *Smolny* that took us, via the North Sea and the Kiel Canal, through Germany to the Gulf of

The Ship *Smolny*.

Sylvi (left) with a Mr. Koivu and a woman on her way to get married.

Finland and on to Leningrad. As I watched the cargo being loaded on the *Smolny* by derrick, our old oat box appeared, swinging crazily in the air for a few seconds before hitting the hold with a thud that caused a whole cloud of oat dust to rise from its cracks. If anyone had asked, I would have said I didn't know whose it was.

Our first meal on the Russian ship was a big surprise. The table was loaded with cold cuts, herring, canned fish, cheese and lots of good bread. We were all hungry, so we cleaned the table pretty well, thinking that was it. Then they proceeded to bring on the main course: chicken with many side dishes and all kinds of goodies. We stuffed ourselves but made a very poor showing, unfortunately, as this was the last good meal we were to see for quite a few years.

Customs inspection in Leningrad took one whole day. We didn't lose anything, but had to open all our luggage, even the oat box which was roped every twelve inches and knotted at every joint. It proved impossible to untie the ropes so I had to cut them all with a knife, and I threw them into a corner in disgust while the indifferent inspector pawed through the contents. Irked as I was, I couldn't help but notice one fellow who breezed through the line without having to open anything. When I got a chance, I asked him what sort of magic he possessed.

"I shook hands with a five dollar bill," he explained.

It seemed that even Marxists were not immune to a little capitalist graft, especially, we discovered, when the bribe was in American dollars. It was a little disappointing to see that this was going on, but of course it wasn't Russia's fault if a few unscrupulous and materialistic workers had gotten in.

We were met in Leningrad by a guide from the Karelian Technical Aid organization whose job it was to take care of us while we were in Leningrad and then send us on to our government-assigned work locations. As we waited to complete customs, we watched some stevedores loading a ship in the harbor, and I commented to the guide that they seemed to be barely moving.

"If you had to do that kind of work with the food they're getting, I doubt you'd do any better," was his terse reply. This made me wonder if the food shortages in Karelia were worse than we expected. We would soon find out.

After customs our guide took us to a hotel where I had my first whiff of a really rank odor that was to become very familiar.

"What the hell smells so bad?" I asked.

It was homemade cigarettes. Although good, factory-made cigarettes were available, they were very expensive, and most people made their own from a tobacco called mahorka which they rolled up in newsprint. The accepted method was to roll a small piece of newspaper into a cone, bend the wide end up forming what looked a little like the bowl of a pipe, and fill that with tobacco. I eventually learned to make them but I never did like mahorka.

The Karelian government was eager to utilize new American techniques of lumbering to harvest the "green gold" of Karelia. Given my experience in lumber camps and in running a saw mill, it was perhaps inevitable that we would be sent to a lumber camp. Sure enough, a few days after arriving in Leningrad, we received a "command" to go north to Uhtua, a town about one hundred miles south of the Arctic Circle.

On the train we became acquainted with the director of a paper mill, the Kontupohja Paperi Tehdäs. He suggested that we get off the train at Kontupohja and come to work for him, but since we had been assigned by the government to work in Uhtua, I didn't see how we could change the plan.

"Are we allowed to come and work for you?" I asked.

"It's a free country," he said. "You can go wherever you want."

We were hesitant. At any rate, our baggage was on its way to Uhtua and we decided we had better go there too. Now, looking back, I am sure that it is a good thing we went where we had been told to go. It wasn't a "free country" over there as we knew the term, and we think it strange now that this factory director would have said it was.

At Kemi, on the western shore of the White Sea, we left the train and rode in the open box of a Ford Model A pick-up truck the 180 kilometers west to Uhtua. One other family from the United States was with us. It was very cold for mid-June with even a little snow that made it feel colder.

Uhtua was a small town on the shore of Lake Keskikuitti (the town has since been renamed Kalevala). It was the commercial center for that part of Karelia. There was no railroad, only a poor gravel road from the Kemi station. The town did have a clinic and hospital, grocery store, schools and the usual government offices. A liquor store was a recent addition; for years Uhtua had been a "dry" town where the state sent drunks to work. There were also docks along the shore for the small ships and tugs that were used for transportation to lumber camps and villages in the summers. Recruits like ourselves came first to Uhtua and then were sent out to the different lumber camps in the area wherever they were needed. We were just a few days in Uhtua before we were taken across the lake about thirty kilometers in a cute little wood-fired steamboat to the Vonganperä Lumber Camp. I enjoyed that trip. I was reminded of the boat later when I saw the movie "African Queen."

Vonganperä had several large barracks and a horse barn that had been built for the time when the timber was being harvested. Now it looked quite deserted as the place was pretty well logged out. All the lumbering and transporting had been done with horses and men; it was hard to believe how much they had accomplished in the three years or so that the camp had been in operation.

The blacksmith shop and blacksmith were still there when we came; he was hammering scythe blades out of steel bars—very thin, narrow and light weight—which were attached to straight wooden handles. The smith was from Finland, and I was told that he was very good at his trade. He also liked his drink, and, when there was no vodka to be had, which was often, he would drink aftershave lotion with a high alcohol content. (Oddly enough, that was usually available.) This brand of lotion had a picture of a reindeer on the bottle so the blacksmith called it *poro rommi* (reindeer rum).

We slept in a log barracks. Each couple had a room to themselves, and they were nice enough but quite full of bed bugs. We had been warned about these back in New York and told to bring some "twenty mule team Borax," a white cleaning powder. I first tried putting some Borax around each leg of the bed* to discourage them but that didn't help at all—we just had white bugs. So next I put water into tin cans and set each leg of the bed into a can. That did help for a while—the bugs were poor swimmers—but pretty soon they got smarter and climbed to the ceiling from which they dive-bombed the bed by air. At least there were less of them. Bedbugs were a constant problem all the time we were in Karelia.

The cooks at Vonganperä were Finnish women so the food was better than average. They baked their own bread, a mixture of wheat and rye that was very good. "This bread is what keeps us on the trail," the men used to say, but after hiking a few kilometers single file the men in the rear would complain about being gassed.

Many trees had been cut down and hauled out the previous winter, and the tops of these had been left lying on the ground. I was given the job of trimming them in order to get all the branches close to the ground

---

*Our hide-a-bed was not shipped up to the lumber camps. We used it later, when we settled in Petrozavodsk.

where they would decay instead of drying out and becoming fuel for forest fires. It also allowed new growth to start sooner. It was a sensible practice, and one I had never heard of before. The accepted method in the United States was to leave the branches and tops where they fell, (except in hardwood forests where the tops were later trimmed and used for firewood, charcoal and chemicals). Perhaps the millions of trees and hundreds of lives lost in the forest fires of Michigan and Minnesota could have been saved had this trimming been done. My pay for this work was ten *kopecks* per tree top. I kept count, and had a hard time making any money. Of course, our room and board were provided so I didn't need much either.

After a couple of weeks of trimming trees at Vonganperä, my hands were full of blisters, and I was glad when we were sent to a new camp called Kannussuo, which was being built about ten kilometers further inland from the lake. Here everybody, men and women, slept together on a raised shelf in a big loft. Sylvi was uncomfortable with the lack of privacy and the crude jokes that were passed around.

My first job there was making shingles with a machine run by man power. It consisted of a large wooden frame from which hung a wooden box filled with sand weighing six to eight hundred pounds. Above the box, the wooden poles suspending it were attached to a steel blade so that swinging the box back and forth also caused the blade to move back and forth horizontally. Each forward motion of the blade sliced a shingle from an eight-by-eight-by-twelve-inch block of pine. Four men stood on the ground swinging the sand box back and forth; a fifth man fed the blocks of wood to the blade. The shingles were about three-eighth-inch thick, cut with the grain. I was told that shingles made this way were superior to those that had been sawed because the saw cut leaves a rougher surface that would not shed water as well as a shaved shingle.

In a few more weeks, some of us were sent out to a grassy area around some small lakes about five miles from Kannussuo to make hay for the horses. We cut the grass with scythes and coiled it onto poles to dry as they did in Finland. The hay was left like that until it was needed in the winter months. There was a small shack at this location in which we kept supplies, but we slept outside on pine boughs with our feet toward the fire. It was quite comfortable after a long day of hard work.

Again we worked as a five-man team. The lead man would be a few feet ahead of the second, who was a bit ahead of the third and so on so we formed a diagonal row (just as the big harvesting machines do in the fields today). In this way, we all had to keep up with the leader and everyone would cut the same amount.

There was also a woman in the camp who did all the cooking on an open fire. One evening she dipped into her personal supply of coffee and made a pot for all of us. It was a real treat. We had all been sitting quietly around the fire but when the coffee came, everyone began to talk. What a difference coffee can make, especially to people who haven't had any for a long time.

I have always enjoyed fishing, so after the evening meal I would venture out to a small lake to fish for perch. I found a log raft someone had made, big enough to hold two or three people, and soon I had an older fellow coming to fish with me. We would pole it out on the quiet lake and fish until it got dark. He had a funny habit of spitting on the fish hook after he baited it and then he would twitch the pole on the surface to attract the fish. I'm not sure if any of this made any difference but we got plenty of very good fish.

We had been there about a week when I told the others that I would like to go back to Vonganperä to see Sylvi. I knew she must be lonesome and I was lonesome for her too. The others said it was okay with them; some even encouraged me to go. One man told me to follow some ridges through the woods until I came to a logging trail that would take me to the camp. About nine at night I took off for the ten kilometer hike. So far up north there was ample light on the trails, although it was difficult to see in the heavy timber. I watched the stars to keep my direction. In about two hours I was at Vonganperä, and Sylvi and I were happy to be together for a little while. The time went so fast. I left early in the morning in order to be back to work, and on the way I met one of the camp bosses. He had come out from Kannussuo to see how our work was progressing and discovered that I had gone to see my wife. He really chewed me out and told me never again to leave work without permission. "It is not done," he insisted. "When you're on a job, you stay there."

The job was more important than family! I kept my cool but I sure felt like telling him off. What an attitude! But this, I thought at the time, was only one man. For the most part, the camp bosses were fair, and morale was high among the workers. Anything you did was noticed and appreciated, and we were all proud of what we had been able to accomplish.

My next job was floating logs to the sawmills down the river at a place called Sakura Järvi. Happily, Sylvi was sent along as cook. We left Vonganperä in a motorboat, eighteen men and Sylvi. All we could do by motor was cross the lake to where the river started; then we had to portage about a quarter mile and put our things into two large rowboats for the rest of the trip. We ate our lunch sitting there on the river bank—some good herring and rye bread—a real treat for me.

The rowboats were about twenty feet long with three pair of oars and a steering paddle in back. After rowing a short distance we stopped at a small village to pick up a young Karelian girl to be a helper to Sylvi. It was probably the first time she had been with Americans and Finns. When she came into the boat she took a rower's seat but the men chased her into the bow with Sylvi. At first she couldn't understand what they meant. When she realized they didn't want her to row she was really surprised.

The camp at Sakura Järvi was another log building with a cook shack attached. Sylvi and I slept in the cook shack the first night and suffered from bed bugs. From then on we retired to the pantry floor where they were less plentiful. The Karelian girl made her bed outside in a large oat box; it was a good choice—no bed bugs.

The weather being very hot, we decided to work at night. It was light enough to see, even at midnight; the only problem was the little black flies or no-see-ums. We used string to tie our pants shut at the ankles and our sleeves tight at the wrists and put scarves around our necks, but the flies still got through somehow, and we were bitten all over our bodies. The bugs were so thick they even got in our eyes and mouths.

The work was very hard there. The logging crews had left fourteen- to twenty-foot pine logs scattered all over as they had had no means to stack them. We ourselves had only axes to work with, and we cut long poles with which to pry the logs and built skids to help us roll them over stumps in order to get them down to the river.

This job had been contracted for a lump sum with Karelles, the largest of three lumber trusts in Karelia. The man in charge of our group, a communist party member named Seppala, had negotiated the price. The eighteen of us had been divided into three work gangs. After a few days work Seppala called us all to a meeting. The purpose of the meeting, he said, was to evaluate each man's worth and decide how much each one would be paid. He would call out each man's name and someone from his gang was supposed to say whether he was one hundred percent productive (did as much work as anyone) or ninety percent, eighty percent or whatever. Those who were more productive would then be paid proportionately more.

Some of the men in our group were older men, and not as strong. There was clearly a difference in what each man was able to do, but who was going to volunteer to make that evaluation when it would result in someone getting less pay? This deal went against the grain with me, and I think with the others too. We had been taught that even though some people weren't physically able to do as much as the others, they deserved full pay if they were doing their best. I believe all of us—Americans and Canadians felt this way. It probably went against party instructions, but we finally decided that every man was one hundred percent productive. Our pay was divided equally.* What happened then was that after a week or so, three of the older men, trying hard to keep up with the rest for their pride's sake, became too sick to work and were taken back to Vonganperä.

My most pleasant memory of the whole job was getting to go for a swim and wash in the river morning and evening.

From Sakura Järvi we went back to Kannussuo and were then sent to a brick factory a short distance away. Here we made use of horse power. Sylvi got the job of driving the horse in a circle to turn the mixer, a rotating paddle inside a large wooden barrel. Meanwhile I shoveled sand and clay into the barrel with just enough water to make a thick mortar. When the mix was ready, I opened a door at the bottom of the barrel and it flowed out. I then carried it in buckets to the brick makers who worked it into molds. It was interesting to watch them. They would shake the mold and tamp it to get the mixture into the corners, then turn it upside down to slip the brick out. It was important that the mixture was the right consistency or they would have trouble getting the brick to slide out of the mold. After the bricks dried they were stacked into a huge circular mound with a hole in it. The others told me that wood would be placed in the hole and set on fire to cure the bricks. In other words, the bricks themselves formed the kiln. Unfortunately, we left before they were fired so I didn't get to see how it worked.

The completed bricks were sent out by truck, but they didn't always make it to their destination. Some of the truck drivers were Karelians, and the trucks that foreigners had brought over were something new to them. They were very proud and excited about how fast they could drive their trucks. With the roads being dirt or gravel, the bricks bounced around in the back and many cracked or crumbled.

After we got back to Kannussuo I had orders to go to Uhtua to dismantle a sawmill and get it ready to be moved to Kannussuo. I made

*During the second five year plan, 1933-1937, Stalin decided that equalization of pay was a "petty, bourgeois" practice. Hosking (156) and Kort (187).

sketches of all the wooden parts while my three helpers unbolted them. Then we loaded them onto skids and hitched horses to drag them through woods and swamps the thirty or so kilometers to Kannussuo. The power plant for the mill was the toughest job; a semi-diesel weighing about two tons, it took a whole week to transport. Meanwhile, the sawyers were cutting the necessary timbers and planks for reassembly of the mill according to my sketches. This two-man team of sawyers, who were from Finland, was fast and skillful. They evidently had worked at the trade a long time. They would roll a log onto supports about seven feet off the ground. Then, with one man on top of the log and the other underneath, they cut with a long saw along a chalkline. With each down-stroke they cut about one inch into the log. The method is called "whip-sawing." I was surprised how accurate the lumber was. They usually made one-inch boards but they could even do half-inch boards.

All the time we were in the lumber camps we had been trying to arrange to move to the town of Petrozavodsk (Petroskoi in Finnish), the capital of the Karelian Republic. Sylvi wanted to go back to school, and I wanted to do mechanical and metal work. We had written to Heino and asked him what to do to get ourselves transferred. Heino worked at the ski factory in Petrozavodsk, and he had gotten some people there interested in me. The factory director was interested because I had considerable experience in auto mechanics and also because of my sawmill work; there was a sawmill connected to the ski factory. Another man who was interested in me was Laine, a musician in the ski factory band, who knew I played the trumpet. Near the end of the summer, Heino wrote to us in Kannussuo suggesting that Sylvi come down and enroll at the Teacher's College. His idea was that if she were already in Petrozavodsk, I would have a better chance of getting sent there. We decided to try it.

I went with her by boat as far as Uhtua (with permission from the boss—they weren't all sticklers to the rules) and there we met two American boys who were truck drivers between Uhtua and Kemi. One of them agreed to let Sylvi ride in his cab. I was glad about that because the weather was cool and sitting in an open truck box for hours could get miserable.

After Sylvi left on the truck, I decided to look for a dentist while I was in town. I had been bothered with a toothache for some time. So I checked in at the local clinic. The nurse there was a big woman who looked like a prize fighter. Her shoulders were wider than mine. She took one look at my tooth and said it had to come out, but the dentist, unfortunately, would not be there that day or the next. I told her my boat would be leaving that evening and asked if she could call the dentist and explain my predicament. She thought about it for a moment and told me to sit in a high back chair. Then she called in another powerful-looking woman and announced that she was going to pull my tooth and the other one should stand by and help. The helper right away got behind me and put a hammer lock on my head while the first one told me to open wide. When I did, she latched on to my tooth with forceps and started pulling. Even though I had decided I was not going to yell, I did, and tried my best to squirm free. I know my hind end came up from the chair but Katinka behind me held on tight, and the nurse kept pulling. I could feel the pain all the way down from my tooth to my seat.

Finally it came out. What a relief! I walked out in a daze, spitting blood, and headed for the liquor store where I bought a half liter of vodka which I took down to the water front. Sitting on a piling I took a couple of pulls out of the bottle and gingerly felt my gum where the tooth had been. It didn't hurt at all anymore and wasn't numb, just a little tender. By evening when the boat left my jaw was back to normal, a result, I believe, of the fact that it wasn't "frozen" and had a good chance to heal. All the vodka did was to relax me. I don't recommend this method of tooth extraction, but if you can stand the pain, it will heal faster.

Later on, in Petrozavodsk, I had to have a tooth capped. Silver was in very short supply at that time; patients provided their own. I gave the dentist an American dime which he sent to Leningrad to process the silver. I then had a silver cap covered with steel on my tooth which I didn't much like because it was so shiny.*

I went back to Kannussuo and continued with the sawmill. When we first tried it out, the power plant was not running right. We tore it apart and found the gaskets leaking. There were no spare gaskets to be had. I remembered having learned in the United States that several layers of newspaper would work in a pinch, so I suggested that we try it, but the young man in charge of the power plant gave me an argument. Machines were expensive and very hard to come by, and he felt responsible for it. He had gone to school to be a diesel operator. He would not help with anything else at the mill, just sat by the engine. If it had been my mill I would have booted him out, but no one there had

*After our return to the States, a dentist in Detroit found this tooth an object of great interest. Later, when it had to be extracted, I asked to keep it as a souvenir, but the dentist claimed he had already thrown it away.

authority to fire him, and anyone who had a little knowledge about machinery was looked upon as someone special. Eventually I convinced him to try the newspaper gaskets, and he even helped me make them. They worked.

I enjoyed running the sawmill but I was worried about how Sylvi was managing. Then came the day that the director called me to his office to tell me there was a command from Petrozavodsk for me to report there to work at the ski factory. "But you don't have to go," he said. He wanted to keep me in Kannussuo and could have arranged it, but I refused to stay. I wanted to be with my wife.°

I learned later that Laine, the fellow from the ski factory band, had approached Kustaa Rovio, secretary of the Karelian Communist Party, and asked to have me transferred to the ski factory. Hearing that I had already been sent up north to the lumber camps, Rovio had first said it was too late and why hadn't I been sent to Petrozavodsk in the first place. But later he relented and went along with the plan.

°Early Communist doctrine included intentional weakening of family ties; marriage and divorce (even bigamy) was easy. Abortion was readily available. Children were encouraged in school to disobey parents who went against communist ideology, and husbands and wives were often assigned to work in different places. However, this family disintegration policy had undesirable side effects: low birth rate and high juvenile delinquency. By 1935, the party was swinging back toward upholding family values. This would turn out to be very helpful to Lauri and Sylvi in the end, as well as at this time (Rostow 110, Timasheff 195).

Reading, Writing and Shooting

S: The summer of 1934 is a blur of conflicting emotions and impressions to me now. We were still newlyweds; this was, in a way, our honeymoon, but in no way could it be compared to a traditional honeymoon. I was very happy to be with my wonderful husband but terribly homesick and lonesome for my father and brothers. It seemed hard to believe that we were even on the same planet, so distant did they seem to be. The world is much smaller today, and people think nothing of hopping from one continent to another. Not so, at that time. Then too, going to the Soviet Union was a very serious step to take, and, in most cases, the immigrant considered it final. We did not think of ourselves as emigres in the true sense of the word as we had left with the idea that this was not necessarily a final commitment; we assumed that a return was possible.

During the two months or so of summer 1934 that I spent in the north of Karelia, I held several odd jobs. Having never done anything but attend school and then teach, I was ill-prepared for any of the work that needed doing at the lumber camps.

While in Vonganperä, I had no work, and since Lauri had been sent to Kannussuo to make hay, I had a very lonely time of it. A Canadian woman was in the room next to mine. She had a lovely voice, and the old Finnish songs she sang increased my feelings of homesickness and nostalgia, for they reminded me of home and dances at the old Finn hall on Sugar Island.

There was another woman at Vonganperä, a crabby, fault-finding Finnish woman of about sixty who didn't help matters any. One day I happened to be wearing my "beach pajamas," a favorite outfit I'd brought from the States. It consisted of a blouse with pants that were tight-fitting at the waist but flared out to about a yard wide at the ankles. When old Crabby saw me, she proclaimed for all to hear that in all her life she had never seen such ugly clothes! Even then we had a generation gap, old and young criticizing each other.

However, after his hay-making stint, Lauri became one of a group of men that was sent to float logs down a river. Seppala, the man in charge, took pity on me and arranged for me to go along with the group as cook. He also found a Karelian girl, Katja, to work as my helper, but the titles could very well have been reversed as far as I was concerned since it wasn't always clear just who was helping whom! Katja was a gentle soul, always willing to do her share and more. She was accustomed to doing men's work as is generally true in societies not as far developed as ours, so she was very much surprised when she stepped into our boat and took her place at the oars, to find that she was not required to row. Our men told her to sit in the bow while they did the rowing. She was thrilled to find that now she could watch the scenery, and many were her exclamations of surprise as we passed scenes she had often passed before but had not had time to see. Katja and I worked well together, and I liked her. Before we parted, I gave her a purse that she had admired. It was a two way purse, white on one side and blue on the other. She had never seen anything like it, although the women in Karelia did use purses at that time.

We cooked in a huge kettle over an open fire. The hardest part of the job was building the fire each morning. Lauri would help me with it. The menu was simple and monotonous: porridge in the morning, usually cream of wheat or millet, soup at noon made of dried potatoes, canned meat and a lot of river water, and the same in the evening. It hurt to see that often the men would have eaten more had we had more to offer, for there were times when the food ran out. We had a certain amount to be used for each meal and occasionally it just was not enough. This would anger the men, but I don't think their anger was in any way directed against the system in general. It was just a more localized reaction to the place and conditions at hand.

Morale was high. The men worked hard and they also enjoyed themselves, as men are apt to do, with small talk and lumberjack humor. This down-to-earth humor was a cause of great embarrassment to me. I had not been accustomed to rough jokes and was often reduced to tears on hearing them. The little schoolmarm had much to learn about the real world out there!

When we returned to Kannussuo I was given a job gathering moss to be used in caulking. I was paid by the weight of the moss. I never did figure out what was more advantageous: to fill the bag with dry moss, which was faster but did not weigh as much, or to pick wet moss in which case it took longer to fill the sack but then it weighed more when full.

Then of course there was the time when Lauri worked at the brick factory, and I was given the job of driving the horse around in a circle. He was hitched to a long pole that turned the mixer that stirred the mortar. The little horse and I went round and round by the hour. The men told me I was foolish to walk behind the horse. "Just stand off to the side and every time he comes around yell at him or give him the switch," they suggested. But I couldn't do that; I wouldn't have been doing my part of the job.

None of these jobs made me feel very important, but at least I was doing something. Evidently I had written to my father about my feelings of inadequacy concerning the work at the lumber camps. Later, my friend Impi wrote me that others had read my letter and concluded that I was dissatisfied and homesick and unhappy. In my answer to Impi I admitted that I was homesick, at times terribly so, but, to quote from my letter, "that doesn't mean that I don't like it here." As with other difficulties and disappointments, we took everything in stride; we had great hopes for the future.

Late that summer, I received permission to enter the Pedagogical Institute (or Teachers' College) in Petrozavodsk, the capital of the Autonomous Republic of Karelia. I was happy about that because it meant going to school again and teaching, but Lauri had no permit to leave the lumber camps so I had to take off by myself. Naturally I was not at all happy about leaving him, but my great love for study and my interest in becoming a teacher again helped us decide. It did not seem fair to separate husband and wife, and this would not have happened back in the States, but we knew when we came that there would be difficulties of all kinds, and we were prepared to do our bit for the country. Then too, we were quite sure that Lauri would be able to follow me soon, for Heino and a friend of his were working together to get him a command to come to the ski factory where they worked.

The trip from Uhtua to Petrozavodsk was a harrowing experience. Lauri had arranged for me to ride with an American truck driver from Uhtua to Kemi, a distance of 110 miles. Although it was only the first of September, it was very cold and windy so I was glad to be sitting in the warm truck cab. But my joy was short-lived. A few miles down the road an Army officer hailed the truck. He motioned for me to get out of the cab and into the truck box. For the rest of the journey, I sat in the box, cold and miserable, while the officer shared the warm cab with the driver. I know the driver, being an American, would not have had it so, but there was nothing he could do about it. The officer had rank and he pulled it; chivalry did not enter into the case.

At Kemi I sat in the railroad station for hours waiting for a train to Petrozavodsk. I had much more baggage than I could handle because I had with me the tools we had brought for our friend Heino. I knew I could not get them into the train by myself so I spoke to a nice-looking young Karelian lad; I gave him three rubles and asked him to help me whenever the train came in. He took my three rubles, and that was the last I ever saw of him. Somehow I managed. I sat for hours on my pile of luggage, fighting sleep. The train came in, and someone helped me on.

Heino met me at the station in Petrozavodsk and took me to my future home. I was to live with Ilmi and Keijo Frilund and their little girl, Irma, who was about four. They had a two-room apartment which was a luxury in Karelia at that time. We had known Ilmi slightly back home; she often spent summers on Sugar Island with friends, whom we also knew. She and Keijo had lived in Chicago; they'd been married in the States but Irma had been born in Karelia.

Back in the United States, Keijo and his mother had been deeply dedicated to the workers' cause, and she was very active among the Finnish radicals in Chicago. But she elected to stay in the States while Keijo and Ilmi took off for the Soviet Union. Keijo was an electrician at the ski factory, and his wife worked there too. He had become a party member soon after arriving in Karelia. It was not easy to join the party, and they weren't recruiting members. A person had to take the initiative to apply and just having been a party member in the United States didn't guarantee acceptance in Karelia.

If an application was accepted, one first became a candidate for membership and attended classes on political theory. Later, if approved, one became a member. There seemed to be no discrimination against women. We knew only a few party members, and a few more who were candidates, but it was something that was not much discussed. Political matters in general were not discussed as freely over there as in the United States. Perhaps it was because there was only one party, and they made all the decisions. We had no choice.

I was very depressed and poor company at that time. There I was, all alone in an alien land, missing Lauri and homesick for my father and brothers. Heino was determined to raise my spirits and made every effort to get me to smile. One evening he took me to an amusement park and stood me in front of the crazy fun house mirror; he was sure I would smile at my silly reflection. I did smile, but mostly for his sake.

The Frilunds lived in ski factory barracks, a complex of half a dozen or so two-story wooden buildings. They were divided into one or two room apartments, to use the word loosely. Almost all of the residents were Finns from the United States, Canada or Finland. Finnish was one of the official languages of the Karelian Republic, along with Russian, so the language barrier was not too solid although most stores and businesses used only Russian.

Ilmi and Keijo treated me well although they had to give up a lot of their precious privacy on my account. I enjoyed school. However, I was unhappy because my husband was not with me. Then, on the eighteenth of October, Ilmi answered a knock on the door and was handed a telegram. She opened it, read it, looked at me and grinned. For some time she just stood there and grinned. Finally she told me what was in the telegram: Lauri was arriving that very day! I was overjoyed. Heino and I met him at the station, and from then on I was much happier.

I had arrived in Petrozavodsk in the beginning of September, in time for the start of the school year. The Karelian Pedagogical Institute was a two-year school that prepared teachers for the secondary or middle school. Although I had taught school back in the States, I did not have the political knowledge required of a Soviet teacher. Then too, I wanted to speak Finnish correctly and fluently, and I wanted to know something of Finnish literature. For these reasons, the Institute was the place for me. It was located across a large field from the ski factory, and I would usually take a path through the field to get to my classes. Most of the students lived in a dormitory called the Internat. It amused those of us who came from further away in town that these dormitory residents were generally the last ones to get to class. All students received a monthly stipend. The students at the Institute were Finns from Finland, Karelians, and those of us from the United States or Canada. We all got along very well; there was no antagonism among us.

I majored in Finnish language and literature. The curriculum also included Russian language and literature, Russian history, pedagogy (the art or science of teaching), philosophy and war study. All the students on this curriculum spoke Finnish, and some knew Russian or Karelian as well. Karelian seemed to be a mixture of the two languages but more closely related to Finnish. A Russian class for those of us who knew no Russian at all was held after school. The German language was on the curriculum when we started classes at the Institute, but, for some strange reason, which we were not told, it was discontinued after only one session.

Since I was on a Finnish language-literature curriculum, my professors were mostly Finns who presumably had come from Finland at some earlier time. Russian literature and history, however, were taught by a Russian and pedagogy by a Karelian.

Finnish language was taught by Professor Salo who was the very picture of an absent-minded professor, with glasses continually slipping down his nose. He had a habit of calling on me to compare Finnish and English grammar and to translate words from one language to another. This was often difficult for me since I knew nothing of Finnish grammar. I had grown up speaking the dialect of the Varsinais-Suomi region of Finland where my parents had been born and raised. Like most dialects, it was far from book language. During the course of my studies I was often amazed to learn how the correct way to speak or write Finnish differed from what I had known at home. To this day I feel grateful to Professor Salo for what he taught me of my mother tongue.

Professor Ruhanen taught us Finnish literature. He was a handsome young man, well-liked by all the class for his easy-going, good-natured personality. Preparations for this class were difficult since few books were available to us. I would often stay up most of the night to finish a novel in order to have it back at school in the morning for someone else to read.

I had never read Finnish literature and found it very interesting. We also read many Finnish translations of English books. All these novels were studied with the class struggle in mind. This was new to me since of course it had not been so in the United States. A story by the nineteenth-century Finnish author Juhani Aho has stayed in my mind. It was called "Train" and told about the reactions of the residents of a small town to the arrival of the first train in their area. I think I remember this story well because I happened to be the only one in class to see the symbolism of the train. It represented the industrial revolution, and the villagers were unhappy and frightened at the prospect of its coming. I was continually amazed to see how the class struggle and the ideology of the working class were brought into each story we studied.

Professor Bazanov taught us Russian literature and history. I did not learn very much in his class because of the language barrier—he knew only Russian. I had to rely on notes taken by some of my classmates who knew some Russian. Professor Bazanov was a dour young man who seldom smiled or joked. He had a crush on Aini, a young Karelian girl in the class, and we teased her about him.

Our pedagogy teacher, whose name I do not recall, was a Karelian who spoke with a heavy accent and seemed to be a beginner in the field of teaching. He had one peculiarity that aggravated many of us; he would mention a particular topic briefly and then say that we would delve into it more fully later on. But the next time he brought it up, he would simply remind us that we had already dealt with the subject! Consequently, we acquired a rather superficial knowledge of pedagogy as practiced at that time in the Soviet Union. One story the teacher told us has stayed with me.

After the revolution much experimentation went on in Soviet teaching. At one point they tried a method in which the children would study one subject from every possible angle. For instance, they studied chickens: their biology, then their history, then the economics of raising them, and literature about them. It didn't go over well. The children grew weary of it and would plead with the teacher to make an end of the chicken.

Our philosophy class was taught in Finnish by Professor Jaakkola, but, since philosophy is not an easy subject in any language, I found it difficult. I understood it at the time but at this late date, I cannot recall much of it. It was, of course, dialectical materialism, which is the philosophy of communism. It was based on Karl Marx's theory, which had the class struggle as its main doctrine. Marx believed that, since the economic forces in the modern world were in constant conflict, the working class needed to unite and bring about social and political changes that would then result in the dictatorship of the proletariat, which would work for and finally achieve communism, a social system based on common ownership of the means of production and equal distribution of the products of industry. (What we had in the Soviet Union at the time was supposed to be the dictatorship of the proletariat.)

One of our classes, "Sotilas Oppi" (War Study), was something new to most of us. It entailed a study of the rifle and its parts and also shooting practice. Our teacher was the typical, tough sergeant type so often portrayed in war movies. One afternoon when we were out for rifle practice, lying on the ground and shooting at paper targets, a breeze came up and caused the targets to move about. My friend Flossie complained about this, to which the old sergeant replied, "The Capitalist Exploiter won't hold his head still either." This was a startling thought; we were preparing for the final conflict!

Although I had heard the words "final conflict" all through childhood, it was a shock to have it brought to my attention in such a realistic way. Were we really preparing to go out into the battlefield and do actual combat with the enemy (the enemy being the capitalist exploiter)? Was I ready for that? It had never occurred to me so vividly before. But, if this was what was needed, then so be it. We had our warfare classes and our target practice. Luckily I never had to make use of it.

The two smartest pupils in our class were a Finnish man named Sampsa Pulkkinen (for fun we would call him Pumpsa Salkkinen but he didn't mind) and a Finnsh girl named Maiju Gylling. Maiju's father was the Chairman of the Executive Committee of the Karelian Republic (the top man in Karelia) when we first went there. Maiju was a little older than most of us, and very intelligent.

A young Karelian lad whose name I do not recall was a constant source of amusement to us. He had witty sayings that he would always quote at opportune moments. Whenever someone became excited, he would caution them, "*Rauhallisuus ennen kaikkea*," (Above all, keep calm). When something needed straightening out, he would say, "*Huonokin järjestys on parempi kuin epäjärjestys*," (Even poor order is better than disorder). We always enjoyed his comments; they are funnier in Finnish. As is true in all languages, something is lost in the translation of proverbs, axioms, etc.

The little group with which I often studied was comprised of Selma Anderson and Flossie Merilä from the States; Inkeri Letonmäki and Lempi, originally from Finland; Aino from Karelia; and Katri Muukkonen, a Russian who had lived in the United States for a few years. Katri had been born in Russia, but in the twenties she had met and married an American Finn who had come to the Soviet Union to work in an automobile factory. When he returned to the States, he took Katri with him, and they lived there for some years, lastly in Detroit, before coming back to the Soviet Union in 1933. Katri was always in our small study group

Class from the Karelian Pedagogical Institute. Inkeri Letonmäki is on the left in the front row. In the middle row, Professor Bazanov is third from the left, followed by Professor Salo. Sylvi is second from the right with Maiju Gylling at the far right. Flossie is in the back row directly behind Sylvi, with Sampsa Pulkkinen next to her.

and did her best to translate Russian into Finnish or English.

None of us in this group lived at the dormitory, and we would get together in each other's "homes" (rooms, actually) to study. Of course, we did a lot of visiting too, and drank coffee if it was available, which was seldom. *Chai* (tea) or *mocha* (coffee made from wheat, rye or other grains) was the common fare. It was a wonderful treat to get real coffee.

At one such gathering I got in trouble with the rest of the group. I have always enjoyed making rhymes and quoting from poets and rhymesters. This time I began to recite what I thought was a cute little rhyme that went thus: "There's nothing new under the sun, nor poem nor pun. . . ." I got no further when the other girls informed me, in no uncertain terms, that this was a decadent, bourgeois way of thinking, and not at all in line with Soviet philosophy. I took heed.

This made me realize how easy it was to think and voice opinions that could be construed to be bourgeois and against Soviet philosophy. According to the Soviet line of thought, they were constantly coming up with new ideas and new inventions, progress in every field, and to say there was nothing new under the sun was indeed wrong. I would do well to think twice before reciting even humorous bits of verse or prose learned earlier in our capitalist environment. They might be misconstrued.

As I have mentioned before, we did not, as a rule, talk politics with our friends. All power came from above, and we soon realized that even constructive criticism was not welcomed and could be misunderstood or deliberately twisted. Politics entered every phase of our lives and, in that respect, life differed greatly from what we had lived back in the States. Of course, our parents had been involved in politics and discussed it among themselves, but Lauri and I had not paid much attention. I, for one, was concerned only with school and the social life connected with it. But in Karelia, each school, each factory, every workplace had its political organizer or teacher. They held meetings regularly at which the workers and students were taught the tenets of communism. They would also hold meetings at the various barracks, and, although attendance was not required, it was what we called "voluntary compulsion"; it was best to go.

Two very important celebrations took place during the school year. One was in honor of the October Revolution of 1917, and the other was May Day, the first of May. Big parades were held on these occasions with the whole town taking part. Students from the Institute met at a predetermined street corner very early in the morning to await our turn in the parade. Much talking and joshing took up our time while we waited. These parades and the speeches we heard were stirring experiences as, of course, they were meant to be. High officials of the Karelian Autonomous Republic, such as Maiju's father, Edvard Gylling, were in the reviewing stand with perhaps one or two from Leningrad or Moscow. They made speeches praising the Communist Party, the workers' government and, above all, Stalin. Stalin was the mightiest of the mighty, a demigod, from whom all blessings flowed, to whom we gave thanks for any and every good we received.*

Stalin had been in power for ten years by this time, and his personality cult had already become very strong. It was cultivated in every possible way. Among ordinary people there was already a feeling that perhaps it was a little bit exaggerated, but we still felt that Stalin was the true ruler of the people and had only our welfare in mind. He was a father figure to all of us. And so we listened to the speeches and hurrahed and applauded at the right times.

---

*A typical song about Stalin went: "We give thee our thanks for the sun thou has lit" (Kort 198). Another was called, "Glory to the Great Name of Stalin" (Randall 118).

In December of 1934, Kirov, a prominent member of the Soviet government, was assassinated in Leningrad. The day of his funeral was a public day of mourning. Zinoviev and Kamenev, also government officials, were arrested and charged with the crime. According to the newspapers, they pleaded guilty. They did not, however, have a public trial at this time.

In 1935 we began to read in the papers about other arrests of government officials. They were accused of being "counter revolutionary" which meant they were against what the Communist Party wanted. The Party was in charge. What the Party said was right, was right. You didn't argue with the Party. That was the system. Party members were thought of as being representatives of the people. They were from the working class (we were *all* working class), and they weren't making any money for their work in the Party—why shouldn't they look after the interests of the people? There seemed to be no reason not to trust the Party to do the right thing. And so it seemed to be a good idea to get these "counter revolutionaries" out of positions of authority, "purging" the Party, as it later came to be known. Of course we had no inkling, at that time, what these "purges" would turn into.

Boats, Trumpets and Piston Rings

L: I stayed at Kannussuo long enough to train an American Finn to operate and take care of the sawmill. Then I too caught a ride in the cab of a truck to Kemi. (Luckily, no officers needed a ride that day.) Arriving in Kemi, I was left at the railroad station with my suitcases and trunks, which included that heavy oat box. I was worried that I didn't have enough money for my ticket plus all the baggage so I asked, in Finnish, at the ticket window how much it would be.

The ticket seller was a young Karelian girl who spoke some Finnish—reluctantly. From what I understood, she told me to purchase a ticket, and then she would tell me what the baggage cost. I tried to explain that I needed to know the full price before I bought the ticket but she slammed the window shut and refused to open it for me. This kind of behavior was typical of many little bureaucrats we were to see later.

I left, looking for help, and met a friendly Karelian woman who understood my Finnish and also spoke Russian. She seemed to be a smart and capable person, and I explained my predicament. With a twinkle in her eye she agreed to translate for me, so back we went to the ticket window where she knocked, producing the same ticket seller. An exchange of Russian followed, of which I understood nothing except the ticket seller's firm "*nyet.*"

My translator wouldn't take that and began to yell, even to spit, at our adversary. Of course, that didn't help, but my Karelian friend was not one to give up easily. With me in tow she scouted around for a policeman, and the three of us returned to face the mistress of the ticket window. There was more heated Russian, but this time the little bureaucrat, red faced and angry, had to come around. I had enough money to buy my ticket and ship all the baggage.

Of course there are petty bureaucrats everywhere who seem to like to hassle people, but it was disappointing to find them over there, because it wasn't supposed to be that way. In a socialist society all workers were supposed to be equal. That was part of the dream.

The train I was to take didn't leave until the following day, so I had to find a place for the night. As it happened, a young Russian army officer came to talk to me. He spoke very good Finnish; I later learned he was a Finn. I asked him about hotels in Kemi, and he invited me to go along with him, and we would get a room together. We sloshed through the muddy streets, he cursing that the place was always muddy whenever he came. He was very interested in the United States and asked a lot of questions. He also wondered how I got stuck in such an awful place as Kemi.

He was in the army, he said, because it was a better life than civilian work and, with his experience, suited him better. I learned later that army food and clothing were much better than what the average worker could get. The next morning after breakfast we returned to the station and sat and talked some more. He was one of the nicest people I met over there—very intelligent and helpful.

When my train came, I got into a compartment with a Russian fellow. Finding my Russian poor, he began with sign language, inviting me to join him for a drink. I was afraid to leave my suitcases but he assured me they were safe. So we drank together and talked, or mimed, in our own way and it was surprising how well we could understand each other.

Across the aisle from me and my friend were about ten men dressed just in rags with birch bark shoes. They were not prisoners but displaced persons, called "*usloni*" in Russian.* They looked pitiful. At that time almost everyone carried their lunch along with them—if they had nothing else they usually had bread. When I finished my lunch of bread and a small tin of fish, one of these ragamuffins pointed to the can. He wanted

*These were probably kulaks; Russian peasants who were torn from their homesteads after the Revolution and told to go and join collective farms. Many starved.

it. There was a little bit of oil left in it. I handed it over and when he was through wiping it with his bread it was completely clean. He thanked me over and over. My Russian friend didn't seem at all concerned at their plight, and that was the general attitude we saw over there toward those people. Those who were better off seemed to think, "Whatever they've done, they probably deserved it. It's not my responsibility." This attitude bothered me.

When I arrived in Petrozavodsk, Sylvi was still living with Ilmi and Keijo Frilund. I moved in, too, for a few months until we got to move into another ski factory barracks a stone's throw away.

The Gylling Ski Factory, named for Edvard Gylling, leader of the Karelian Republic, employed about 250 workers. It was the second largest factory in town, the biggest being Onegzavod, where cast iron and steel castings were made. Located on the shore of Lake Ääninen (Onega in Russian), the ski factory had a wood-fueled power house, a lumber yard to store the bolts* that the skis were made from, a heated kiln for drying, and a sawmill to cut the bolts and material for the woodworking shop. There was also a small machine shop where cutters were made and machines repaired. The whole area (except for the lake side) was surrounded with a wire fence about ten feet high, and there were watch dogs on long wire ropes patrolling inside the fence. The one entrance was guarded day and night. You couldn't just walk in; if the guard didn't know you, you had to show your pass.

The director of the ski factory, Elias Tuomainen, was from the Savo region of Finland. He had been in Karelia for years, since shortly after the Revolution. He wanted to know if I had any experience on auto and marine engines which, of course, I had, having operated and repaired marine engines on the St. Mary's River since I was twelve years old. He was having a boat built for the ski factory by an American boat builder from Oregon, another immigrant to Karelia, who had been a commercial fisherman on the Columbia River. (I think his name was Kari.) The craft he was building was about twenty-eight feet long and modeled like the Columbia River boats were at that time. To me it was just beautiful, and subsequently proved to be seaworthy as well.

The ski factory had an old six-cylinder automobile engine that they hoped to repair and use in the boat. It was an Oakland engine just like

---

*A bolt of wood is a one-quarter lengthwise section of a log. Skis were made from the outside of the log, always with the bark side down because that side had a tendency to form a natural arch which is good on the bottom of a ski.

one I had had in 1928 on an old Oakland four door. They told me to check it out and give them a list of parts to be replaced. I did and it was a long one, including pistons, piston rings, valves, plugs, springs, gaskets, and more, none of which were ever procured. "Do the best you can," I was told.

The director's brother, Arne Tuomainen, was shop foreman. "We can make the piston rings and valves in the shop," he told me. I gave the lathe hand the size for the rings; he turned them; we peened the inside for tension, cut and fitted them in place. It was quite an experience for me. We decided to use the old pistons, but we even made a new propeller, welded construction. It worked very well.

The propeller shaft extended from the stern to the engine, which was mid-ship, and was uncovered—at first. One day while I worked on the boat with the engine running (and the shaft turning), I stepped quickly over it and one leg of my pants caught on a set screw and immediately started to wrap around the shaft. I grabbed the cabin wall and hung on for all I was worth. There was a ripping sound, and I found myself standing there with only one leg on my pants. The other one was torn off at the waist and wrapped around the propeller shaft. My leg was okay—just scratched a bit—but I had to go home for another pair of pants. After that I built a box around the prop shaft.

I worked off and on between the boat and machine repair all winter. Then in the spring when the ice went out we put the boat in Lake Ääninen, a fairly large body of water.

It took me a couple of days to get the motor started and then it was running on only four or five cylinders. All the spark plugs were old, and I kept changing them around. One day the director came out to the boat to ask how I was doing. I told him it wasn't running well, and we needed better plugs. He listened to the motor but, undaunted, said we would take the boat to a neighboring village about twenty-five miles away and get some fish for the ski factory cafeteria from the kolkhoz* there. "We'll leave tomorrow afternoon," he said, "and stay overnight."

We had only tried the boat a couple of times, and the motor was still very tight. I worked on it late that night and early the next morning. It was still not right when we started out on the open lake, but after about two hours of coaxing the engine finally took off on all six. What a difference! Now we were doing fourteen to fifteen miles an hour, and soon were at the village where we were invited in to eat at the home of the

*A collective farm.

kolkhoz director. I felt bad because my clothes were oily and dirty, but I needn't have worried; they draped a white sheet over each of us before serving. (Of course then I worried about getting the sheet dirty!) The first course consisted of water that fish had been boiled in. Next we had the boiled fish with sour bread and tea.

Meanwhile the wind had picked up and was blowing quite a gale. We went to bed hoping the storm would let up during the night. It didn't look too bad in the morning, so we shoved off. We had a head wind and ran at half speed. I was afraid to pound the boat any harder. The weather kept getting worse, and we were making very little headway.

Tuomainen asked me if I thought the engine would keep running, and I told him that at the rate we were going we wouldn't have enough fuel to make it. So we turned back to the village, and he telephoned back to Petrozavodsk to send us some fuel as soon as the weather permitted. A small diesel tug arrived that afternoon but had no fuel for us. Instead, they started to tow us back, which made Tuomainen very unhappy. He asked me to let him know when we were close enough to make it with the fuel we had. As soon as I gave the word, we were off, leaving the tug behind and beating them in by half an hour. Tuomainen was really pleased, and I felt better too.

The ski factory had a restaurant located outside the fence, with two eating areas, one for technical personnel and the other for workers. I never had the pleasure of eating with the technical people, but I was told by some that they had better food. In our area, the mainstay of the meals was sour bread, and we often had cabbage soup and very little else. Sometimes there was a bit of meat in the soup. I was lucky because I like cabbage soup. I used to keep ladling it away, telling the others how good it was for them, but nobody would buy that. I just got dirty looks.

There was a little beer kiosk about a quarter mile from our barracks. The place was so small that only five or six people could stand inside; some got their drink and went outside to drink it. I would take a bucket there, get it filled, and drink it at home. One time I remember when I was having my bucket filled that there was a man inside with his eight- or nine-year-old son; they were drinking beer together. The son looked like quite a little man as he raised his mug and said, "*Davai Papa vypim*" ("Come on Papa, let's drink"). Somehow it struck me so funny that I remember it to this day.

Life went along smoothly. Sylvi went to school and I continued to work in the ski factory machine shop where I was soon made foreman of machine repair. I liked it, although I was on call day and night if there was any problem the shift workers couldn't handle. Of course this was overtime, which meant more money; sometimes I would more than double my salary. I also got bonus checks for improvements in the machines. If the improvement eliminated one worker, they would pay a certain percent of the savings.

The ski factory also had a section where they built furniture—tables, chairs, cabinets, and other pieces—mostly of birch with some poplar and pine. The machines—planers, saws, and trimmers—were primarily Swedish made, some Finnish and some American. (I seem to remember one saw that was stamped Three Rivers, Michigan.) Many of these things had probably been brought to Karelia by recruits like us, but the Russian government did send buyers to the United States and possibly to other countries as well.

The skis, mostly for cross country, were birch and very well made under the direction of Snellman, a Finnish engineer who had been with the factory from its very beginning, some time in the early twenties. The ski machinery was all of his design, made in Sweden, and very efficient.

After I had worked there awhile, I was sent to Moscow along with some of the engineers and foremen to look over another ski factory. As I wrote in a letter to my sister back in Michigan:

> It's a bigger outfit than ours, but the quality of their skis was poorer than ours. We make good skis. Wanna buy a pair?

There were some apprentices at the factory learning to do the handwork on the skis. At first I thought they were only about twelve or thirteen years old, but I was told that none of them were under sixteen. They were small because they had been born during really hard times and hadn't gotten enough food for growth.

One morning the head engineer at the ski factory, a Russian, came to me wanting to know if I knew anything about diesel engines. He had gotten a call from a school that their power plant was out of order. I thought maybe I could help, so we went to take a look at it.

The power plant had a big single-cylinder semi-diesel for generating enough energy to light up the school dormitory and several buildings around. The operator was a Finnish lady; her husband had died, and she had inherited his job. After talking to her I realized she was well qualified. She told me the rod bearing had burned out. We tore down the engine, took the bearing back to the ski factory and poured a new one out of babbit. After we fitted it in and started up the engine I was satisfied that the job was done, but the operator kept checking the oil and saying it just didn't act the way it used to. We waited a couple of hours, then left telling her to call if she had any trouble. The following morning she did, telling us that the engine was knocking loudly and the bearing was burned out. We went back and did the job over again, fitting the new bearing as perfectly as we knew how. She was still skeptical, saying the foam on the oil didn't look right, but I assured her it was a good bearing and she shouldn't worry.

The same thing happened again: there was the phone call and the plant was down again with no electricity. This time we tore that engine down so we could inspect every moving part. Finally one of the men asked me why a certain copper tube was bent. There was the problem. The tube was the source of oil for the crank; because of the bend in it, the rod bearing wasn't getting the full amount of oil. We corrected it and this time when we started the engine up again the operator was happy. The foam on the oil was the way it should be.

I got extra pay for that job, and the engineer got a new bicycle that he had wanted from the school management. I like to think we saved the lady's job.

There was always need for machine repair at small woodworking shops in town, so I decided to do repair work evenings and weekends along with Keijo Frilund who was an electrician. I knew this kind of thing was frowned upon, but Keijo was a Party member so I figured it was probably okay.* At first we found it difficult to get a decent price; the people just loved to haggle, and we would end up cutting our price and making very little. After we got onto their ways, we started making our first bid about forty percent higher than what we wanted and then we did quite well. We allowed our customers to chew us down quite a bit, which made them happy, but we still had a comfortable fee for our services.

One of the things I liked most about the ski factory was their brass band. As I mentioned, one of the reasons I got to go to the ski factory was because I played the trumpet. I started right in practicing with the group.

Laine, a baritone player, was the best musician in our band. He had learned to play in the Russian army. Before the Russian revolution when Finland was under Russian rule, Finns were conscripted into the Russian army. They also took young boys with musical talent and taught them to

---

*It was *not* okay—officially. Private enterprise employing hired labor was considered a crime with which there could be no compromise. (Dallin 8).

The ski factory band. Lauri is second from the right in the back. Laine is on his right.

Lauri, honored as a *Stakhanovist*.

play. They had to learn to march and play under all kinds of conditions, even on horseback. Finns called them "battalion players." They had to be good in order to graduate. Laine was one of these.

I started out playing the trumpet and later switched to baritone, which suited me better. There were about twenty-five of us in the band, and we practiced every week. Occasionally we even played in a combined group of bands from all over the territory with about a hundred and fifty musicians. The director of this large group, Teplitsky, was an amazing man. There was talk that he had been a prisoner building the White Sea canal.* He could pick out individual players if they sounded a sour note and make them play a part over again. I had a hard time hearing my own horn.

Elis Ranta was the leader of our ski factory band. We were called upon to play at dances, parades, an occasional concert, and various affairs at the ski factory club. We received no pay for this; it was a civic duty, and one we enjoyed. But we did get paid for playing at funerals. Often, when people had a death in the family, they would hire a band to play the funeral march while the body was being taken to the grave. We would walk directly behind the pallbearers playing slowly in time with our walking. When we got to the grave we would usually go to one side and wait to see if we were needed. There would be a lot of wailing and crying; the women would throw themselves on the grave and carry on for some time. Then they would ask everyone to come to their home for food and drinks, usually plenty of both. I was always amazed at how much food they were able to serve since everything was in short supply.

Once when we were taking a Jewish man to his grave I noticed that his head was rocking from side to side in time with the music. I nudged the guy next to me and pointed it out, and we both grinned. The Jewish grave was different from most. There was a narrow trench dug at the bottom just big enough for the body with a ledge on each side. After the body was put in they laid boards on top so the earth was not thrown directly on the body. They never buried the coffin so they could use it again.

Often we were asked to play at doings some distance from town.

*The 142-mile White Sea to Baltic canal project was assigned in 1930 to Henry Yagoda, notorious head of the secret police. Between 1931 and 1934 the canal was built at the ridiculously low cost of 95,000,000 rubles using 300,000 prisoners from labor camps who worked eleven-hour days on twenty-nine ounces of bread, watery soup and salt fish (Dallin 198). According to Michael Kort (179) it was a "tragic fiasco" costing at least 250,000 lives and then "too shallow to serve its strategic objectives."

We would ride on trucks with some benches in the back so the older folks could sit while the younger ones stood. On rough roads standing was sometimes easier. There was no place to put the instruments so everyone took care of his own. What with hanging on to your instrument and keeping your balance in the truck it was not the most pleasant ride, but we had fun just the same.

Once we went to a Karelian village about a two-hour ride from Petrozavodsk for a young man's funeral. This time we were taken directly to the large old house where he had died. The body was in a coffin to one side for viewing, and a large table was in the middle of the room just loaded with food and glasses of vodka. There weren't enough chairs so we all stood up to eat and drink. The glasses of vodka must have contained about six ounces. I took one and drank it right down, Russian style, and immediately took some sour Russian bread, as was the custom, and sniffed it before eating it. I was talking to someone on my right and didn't notice when my glass was filled up again. When I saw another six ounces of vodka, I asked the fellow what I should do.

"As long as you drink it," he said, "they will fill it up again."

I just left it full.

On this occasion, the funeral procession came after the food was served. I think it was better to have it the other way, because some of the boys drank too much, and we didn't sound as good as usual. Besides that, the road we had to walk was full of ruts and holes. It was a good thing we all knew our notes; it would have been impossible to follow music. Our director was not very happy with us. (He didn't drink.) We did not go back to the house after the burial—it was straight home for us.

One night after the ski factory band had played at some doings, we stopped at a beer garden that was housed in an old church in Petrozavodsk that the state had taken over. We had a hard time talking to each other as we sat with our drinks, because the sound of our voices would go high up in the tower and then bounce back. With forty or fifty people all talking at the same time it was really weird. It did not help to talk louder, in fact, the louder the talk, the more confusing it became.

There were no rest rooms in this place, only outhouses. When I ventured out I heard loud swearing coming from the toilet. Curious, I opened the door. What a sight that was. The toilet was filthy, as they usually were over there, and a drunk had been sliding and falling all over the place. He was a real mess, and he kept swearing in Finnish about how bad it smelled. I just went back to the beer garden, but somehow the beer did not interest me anymore, and I soon left.

One day at band practice Laine asked me if I would like a job repairing some instruments for a lumber camp band. I was agreeable; a little extra money was always nice. He said he knew how, and we would work together on them in the evenings. We sat for many an evening straightening, cleaning and repairing horns. It was interesting work. I had to scrounge around for different-sized ball bearings, used ones. We would break the rings and salvage the round balls which would be pushed through the various tubes on a horn until all the kinks were out. Sometimes the valves would have to be hammered out, they were so corroded, and then soaked in kerosene, sanded, polished and buffed until they looked like new.

We were almost finished when the expeditor from the lumber camp came to see them. He was so pleased, he said, and wanted to take them back with him except for the few that weren't finished yet. He would pay for the whole job when he returned to get the rest. He had been drinking, so we didn't trust him. Laine said no, but after some argument he let the fellow take a couple to show to the camp director. Some weeks later he stopped by again and asked us to deliver the horns to a certain house, and he would pay then.

"Nothing doing," said Laine. "You deliver the cash, and *then* we will deliver the horns."

He did finally come up with the cash, and we brought the horns to a house where he was staying. The lady of the house let us in, and we found him sitting at the table chewing away on a chicken with several children watching. I could see the kids were hungry and undernourished, but the fat slob ignored them and continued to crunch away, grease dripping down his chin. It was a depressing sight, and we were glad to get out of there.

I was earning more than twice the average income. It all went for food and drink and an occasional ticket to a theater or show. I could just imagine how difficult it was for a family with a few kids to get along. I remember a time when the lady who did our wash came over for coffee. We had cookies, and when we put butter on them, she was horrified at our extravagance. She was a good worker and so was her husband, but they had four or five children, and it was tough going.

We had shop meetings at the factory where we would discuss various projects and plans. Shortly after I went to work there, we learned that the factory fire department had decided to cover all the steam heating pipes with metal to make them safer. I thought that was unnecessary and a stupid idea and said as much at one of the meetings. Nobody said anything in reply, either to agree or disagree, and I wondered why. Later Heino told me that he had heard about my remarks from someone in the Party. I had criticized someone in authority. "Don't do that," he warned me, "It isn't healthy."

That scared me. They claimed that they had freedom of speech in the Soviet Union. It was in their constitution. But going against the Party was something different. If you said anything against the Communist Party, you didn't deserve to be protected by the constitution. You had to go along with the Party, and it just seemed to follow that you weren't supposed to criticize anyone in authority. This was hard to take.

Everything came from the top down, even more so than in the United States. This wasn't at all what we had expected. We knew the revolution was built on the idea of a dictatorship, but it was supposed to be a dictatorship of the proletariat. The workers. Us! We were supposed to be running the show. But I guess we hadn't really thought it through, because a dictatorship couldn't possibly be run by everybody. Some small group had to have the real power, and over there it was the Communist Party. So I began to learn to keep some of my opinions to myself.

At Home on Swamp Street

S: We lived with the Frilunds through the winter of 1934-35 and then, early in the spring, were able to get a room for ourselves in another ski factory barracks, on *Bolotnaya Ulitsa* (Swamp Street). It was a very small room (having originally been intended for a toilet) but we were overjoyed to be by ourselves—I even enjoyed keeping house.

The barracks had no running water. A barrel of water was hauled to the back yard every day in a horse drawn wagon. When it arrived, the driver would come into the barracks, yelling, "*vodi, vodi*;" everyone would then rush out with a bucket and get his share. We did not have to pay for it. Slop water went into a bucket in the room and was carried out and dumped into a pit in the back yard.

Our first place was a little corner room and very difficult to heat; many nights the water would freeze in our buckets right in the room. Our stove, which we used for heating as well as cooking, was made of brick with a metal plate on top and used wood for fuel. The fire would go out during the day and have to be lit when we got home at night. Then it would go out at night and have to be lit in the morning. We were on our own as far as getting wood, sometimes using slabs from sawmills or trimmings from the ski factory, which we had to collect and carry up to the room. With time we learned how much wood to use and how to operate the draft to keep the fire going all night. Our Hudson Bay blanket came in handy at this time, as well as a lamb's wool comforter that had been made by Mrs. Lahti, a neighbor of ours in Michigan, and was very warm but lightweight. We lived in this small room for only a few months and then succeeded in getting a bigger, sunnier one on the second floor of the barracks.

Besides our hide-a-bed, we had plain but adequate furniture made at the ski factory. The walls of the room were papered. At that time green was my favorite color, and I managed to have so much of it in the room that it evoked comments from friends who came over. Hanging above our bed we had a picture of a baby. Lauri's sister Irja had drawn it for us—to serve as a sample, she said. We also had a lovely snow scene taken at a friend's home on Sugar Island. It hung on another wall. Above the dresser we had pictures of my friend Impi, my brother Andrew, and Ingrid Middleton, our friend in Detroit. On the dresser were more pictures from America. I made curtains of cheesecloth (brought from the United States) with green trim for the one window in the room. This window was in the only outside wall we had. It was of good size, made up of many small panes, one of which opened on hinges to form what was called a *fortochka* in Russian, used for ventilation.

Our privies were outdoors, five of them for the whole barracks, in a row over a huge box. Occasionally, this box would be emptied. A stout-hearted man would come along with a sturdy little horse pulling a large wagon, which some of us dubbed the "gold wagon." He had a bucket attached to the end of a long pole with which he would empty the contents of the privies into the wagon. Then he would sit on his wagon with a hunk of black bread and a bottle of vodka beside him on the seat and cart his load out of town to some predetermined spot. His way out of town led him right by the Pedagogical Institute, and one warm, sunny day in early summer, when we had all our classroom windows opened to let in the fresh air, his wagon overturned just below us—an event which was immediately and sickeningly evident to all. We closed the windows as quickly as possible. It took days for the aroma to vanish from the vicinity during which time we bravely endured the closeness of the classroom rather than let in the tainted springtime air.

L: At Barracks 50 there was originally a toilet planned for each end of both hallways, but when the Finns and Americans moved in they used these rooms for people to live in. One reason they weren't left as toilets was that they would have smelled (the building had no running water); another was to make more room for occupants. They then built the five outside toilets and assigned each one to a group of four families. We would wash them down every day with each family taking their turn at this chore for a week at a time. It happened that it was our turn at latrine duty when a Russian family moved into the barracks and became a part of our "group." When I went to clean I could see that someone had been standing on the seat and missed the hole. I decided I'd better have a talk with them. I explained that we cleaned carefully every day and wanted it kept that way. Apparently the Soviet government had recently had a campaign in which they warned people not to sit on toilet seats for fear of catching infectious diseases. I don't know why they didn't think of telling them to wash the seats and keep them clean. Anyway the Russian family caught on right away; there was no more crap on the seat and they took their turn washing and cleaning. A few months later, another Russian family moved in and the same thing happened, but this time the first Russian came to me cussing the "dirty Russians" who soiled our toilet. Then he added, "I'll take care of it." And he did.

Some time later, a lady health inspector came to our building. She was seen walking the halls with her nose in the air, sniffing, and asking, "*Gdye ubornaya*?" (where is the toilet?). When she was shown, she couldn't seem to understand why they didn't smell, but she was satisfied that there was no health hazard.

There was (and I gather there still is) a chronic shortage of toilet paper in the Soviet Union. We usually carried paper, mostly newsprint (there were no Sears catalogs of course). Once when I had to go to the outhouse from the ski factory yard and was without a supply, I asked the Chief Engineer for some. He took out his notebook and tore out one sheet, about two inches by five. I held my hand out for more and he gave me one more sheet. I had to make that do. Of course people often got caught without and so you saw brown streaks on the walls inside the toilets—they had done the best they could without equipment.

Many of the rooms we lived in also had brown streaks on the walls; these came from killing bedbugs, a constant pastime. I remember a newly arrived young fellow from Chicago, familiar with the bedbug problem, was amazed when he first saw the streaks in the outhouse.

"*Voi saatana, onko täälläkin luteita*?" ("What the devil, are there bedbugs in here too?") he asked. We repeated the remark often, whenever we needed a good laugh.

S: The room at 50 Swamp Street was our home for the next six years. We were comfortable there. We had privacy of a sort, but the walls were thin and family secrets hard to keep. The other residents in the building were, for the most part, a friendly and well-meaning group.

Our closest friends were Eino and Sylvia Dahlstrom who lived in the room right below us. Lauri became acquainted with Eino at the Ski Factory garage where Eino worked as a mechanic. I didn't get to know Sylvia well until after I had graduated from the Institute and was at home more, but, after that, we were often together. Many were the evenings when we would signal each other with a thump of the broom handle on the floor or the ceiling and get together. Their beautiful baby had died in infancy from some digestive disorder, so they were childless just as we were at this time.

Miriam and Benny Laine were also very close friends, although we did not see as much of them as we did of the Dahlstroms. For one thing, they did not live at the Ski Factory Barracks. Like many others, they had come to Karelia with their parents. They had a baby born to them who almost died before the doctor discovered that she was unable to get nourishment from her mother.

Irma and Urho Hill were often in our group. Urho was a Canadian, an electrician. Irma was an American and had a job tarring skis at the ski factory. They married in Karelia and had a baby girl born in the fall of 1937. Before the baby's birth, a group of us decided to help Urho and Irma select a name for it. Each of us put a name into a hat. When the winning slip was pulled, it turned out to be the one Lauri had put in. . . . "Nelda." He had used the first names of both grandmas, Ida and Helen, to form it. The girl is Nelda to this day.

Lauri's cousin Lily and her husband, Dave, were also with us often. They lived on the other side of Petrozavodsk where Dave worked in a blacksmith shop. They were a few years older than we were, but we had fun together.

Miriam and Benny Laine.

Then there were Mary and Eino next door. Mary and her first husband had come to Petrozavodsk several years earlier. Her husband had been killed in an accident, and she then married Eino. Mary was one of the best-natured women I have ever met, with never a harsh word about anyone. Even when she gossiped, it was never malicious.

Next to Mary and Eino lived John and Inkri Saari. They were already middle-aged. Inkri was a small, cheerful lady who always had a witty story to tell. Her husband John was more staid but yet a likeable sort. John Kulmala, an American Finn married to a Karelian, was also in the building. Many American and Canadian men married Karelian girls; the girls obtained better food norms as wives of recruited workers, and the men were proud of their young brides. Viktor Viiki, whom we had known on Sugar Island, married a young Karelian girl in Petrozavodsk and was very proud of the fact.

Across the hall from us lived Aili Salo with her daughter Lillian and son Richie. Lillian was a few years younger than we were, and we did not get to know her very well. Richie was even younger, but since he played cornet in the ski factory band, we knew him well, and he was with us a lot. Whenever his money ran short, he would come to us. Lauri was apt to refuse him, so Richie would come to me, knowing I would help him out.

The librarian from the ski factory also lived in our barracks. He had come from Finland several years earlier and already knew Russian quite well. His wife was a haughty, supercilious Russian who not only ironed her pillowcases both inside and out but also pressed her husband's socks. Since we were not supposed to use electricity except for lights, she was certainly going out of her way to disobey orders. When I rather proudly told her of the progress I had made with my new Russian-Finnish dictionary, she pooh-poohed my accomplishment and said her husband knew every word in the book. This woman probably resented foreigners, for she seemed to enjoy putting me down. I had had two sweaters knit by a Finnish woman out of yarns we brought from America. The sweaters were well made and very nice looking, but this woman took time to tell me one day that while they did look rather nice from a distance, a closer view showed how cheap looking they actually were. However, she could not stop me from enjoying the sweaters, which I brought back with me and wore for some time here in the States.

The ski factory had several barracks forming a complex. Our barracks had twenty rooms with a family in each one. It was a two-story building with a door and stairway near each end and a hallway running the length of each floor. Some of the people kept goats, and in the summer when the outer doors were open, it was not uncommon to meet a goat or two on the stairs. When this happened to me, I would backtrack and take the other stairway.

The goats were stubborn, obstinate animals. In the ski factory area we had wooden sidewalks, raised about six inches or so from the ground. The goats would often be seen walking along these. Meeting one head-on, most people would give way and step off the sidewalk. I, for one, would go far out of my way to avoid the critters. Lauri, however, would stand his ground until they got off the sidewalk. Once he even booted one down the stairs at the barracks. It looked back up at him reproachfully as if to say, "Why did you do that?"

Gypsies were another annoyance that occasionally descended upon us at the barracks. They reminded me of a big flock of black birds. If we saw them first, we would lock our doors. If not, they would push their way in and, in return for money, food or most anything, tell our fortunes. They were very aggressive and would not take no for an answer. I once had an elderly gypsy woman come in; she came right up to me and, as I backed away, she followed me, poking her bony finger into my chest as she foretold my future: I would live to be eighty years old, and I would have two husbands in my lifetime.

The gypsies were very quick to steal if you did not watch them closely. The women wore long black dresses and shawls under which they could hide pilfered items. I do not recall ever seeing men in their groups, and I think gypsies in general had women do this part of the "work."

With housekeeping a difficult chore at best, most of us were not sticklers. One of the worst chores, if not the worst, was trying to keep the cockroaches at bay. Since they moved with ease from room to room, it was a never-ending task. Bedbugs were slightly more controllable. The memory of one woman who lived in the complex has stayed with me. She was a Mrs. Mattson who had emigrated from the United States and brought with her the one-day-a-week cleaning habit. Her room was always spic and span. She even changed the towels each week on that day. I also remember her for this quote: "If a man drinks, it is because of the woman's laxity." Since drinking was common among us at that time, it put the burden of the problem on the women.

I did my own cleaning and cooking which was very simple, but an elderly Finnish woman living in the barracks did our washing. She had four children whose names all began with "T": Tarmo, Taisto, Toivo and Taimi. She would stop in for tea, or coffee if we had it, when she came for our clothes. She was the lady who was so horrified to see us put butter on our cookies—how extravagant! This was during our first year when we were still able to buy from a store called "INSNAB"* which sold only to foreigners and had a bigger selection than was available elsewhere. Later on, when this store was closed, we no longer put butter on cookies.

We usually bought our evening meal at the Ski Factory cafeteria until it burned down. Meals were very simple and varied little from day to day, but we had enough to eat, and it was surprising how eagerly we looked forward to them.

Coffee was a wonderful treat for us all, since it was so seldom available. When we did get some it was in the bean and, often as not, raw. We would then roast it in a pan on the stove, stirring it constantly as it had a tendency to burn easily. In those days we liked our coffee very strong so we felt the lack of it deeply but also found it a great pleasure when we did have some.

We had an electric hotplate but we were forbidden to use it in the barracks; we could use electricity only for lights. To get around this, I had placed our suitcase on the big trunk we had in our room and kept the electric plate in the suitcase. If someone came around while I was making coffee, I would remove the pot from the plate and quickly close the suitcase. Some of our friends found this amusing. We could hide the plate but no one could make coffee in secret: whenever anyone was lucky

*INSNAB was an acronym for *inostrannyy snabzheniye* which means "provisions for foreigners."

enough to have coffee to make she would soon find unexpected company at her door, coaxed there by the tantalizing smell of the freshly-made brew.

Shopping for food in Soviet Karelia at this time differed greatly from what we'd known back home. Aside from the fact that very little was available in the stores and we stood in queues for hours to get whatever was for sale, there was the matter of packaging. This was entirely up to the customer. The stores had no wrapping paper, no bags, no boxes. If we expected to get flour or cereal or sugar, we would take our home-sewn cloth bags in which to carry it home. For meat, the daily newspaper would do. Empty vodka bottles were fine for oil (sunflower seed) or milk. For beer (*piva*) or *kvass* (a Russian malt drink) a bucket was best. Loaves of bread came unwrapped and you did what you could. I once saw a woman pull off her slip right in downtown Petrozavodsk and wrap a loaf of bread in it. But packaging was not important. The main thing was to get something, anything.

We had very little room to store our groceries either. Lauri built a small storage cupboard on the wall in the hallway next to our door. Several people had cupboards in the hallway; they all had locks on them but things did disappear. Lauri made a strong door on ours and then drilled a hole in the wall from the inside of our cupboard into our room. Then he put a heavy leather thong on the cupboard door, put it through the hole and hooked it to a stout spike in our room. We always had to unhook the cord in the room before opening the cupboard door, but we never lost anything from that cupboard.

During part of our stay in Karelia we were buying milk from an elderly Russian lady. She was a lovely person, stately and very lady-like; I felt she must have been an aristocrat before the revolution. At times she would bring the milk to us; sometimes I would go for it. She lived in a small house with gingerbread trim on the eaves. It was always neat, and I remember the bed had several pillows piled high. She had a cow but goat's milk was also much used. We paid a ruble for half a liter of milk and brought it home in empty vodka bottles. We did not squander it. One morning at breakfast we had a shot glass full of milk between the two of us. I had made porridge and we made do.

Since our diet was so very simple, anything extra was apt to be of great importance. A simple cake was cause for great joy. One incident has stayed in my mind. It happened while we were living with the Frilunds. When I came home from school one day, I found no one there but saw that a cake baked by Ilmi before leaving was on the table. I

Keijo and Ilmi Frilund with little Irma.

helped myself to a piece of it, and it was wonderful. Little Irma arrived soon after, but I knew that Keijo would be home at any moment, and I felt that, since the cake had so much meaning for all of us, he would prefer to serve it to Irma himself. Alas, I was wrong. He was quite provoked with me for not having served Irma already. I never did explain to him just how I had felt and why I did as I did.

Another treat in our diet was whipped pudding made of lingonberry juice and cream of wheat. We would cook the juice, sweeten it with sugar (if we had it) or with hard candy (if we had it) and thicken it with cream of wheat. To whip it, we would use a homemade whisk of small twigs. The juice had to cool fast so we would take the bowl into a snowbank, meanwhile whipping vigorously. Potato flour could also be used to thicken the pudding. On a few occasions we made our own by grating the potato, letting it settle and then pouring off the liquid and letting the remaining flour dry.

The lingonberries were picked in the fall—a chore which Lauri took care of each year—and kept in barrels in an outside shed. They would freeze in winter and sweeten a bit. I loved eating the frozen berries although they were still quite tart if no sugar was available. Sugar, when we did get it, came in large chunks of odd sizes and shapes. We had small scissors specially made for cutting sugar.

Our clothes were far from fancy, but they were serviceable. It was amazing how little would satisfy us when we saw that our neighbor had no more than we had. Some Americans and Finns brought more in the way of clothes than others, but no one was richly dressed. I think it would have been, and sometimes was, resented by some of the natives. I had brought with me a cloth coat with a mink collar which I had purchased when I was teaching school. One day I was standing in a queue, wearing this coat, when I noticed a Karelian man eyeing me. I thought no more about him until a Karelian woman spoke up and began to berate him. She told him he had no business giving me such dirty looks; I had come by my clothes honestly and was entitled to them!

I also remember a good looking Finnish girl at school who appeared one day in a full-length muskrat coat. She had an aunt in America who had sent the money with which Maire had bought the coat. No one seemed to envy her her good fortune.

Through the Institute one winter I was able to buy what we then called a snowsuit. It was brown suede-type material: the pants were form-fitting, up to the armpits and had shoulder straps and elastic at the ankles. The jacket was short and also form-fitting. The style was popular with sportsmen over there. I also had felt boots with leather soles and heels. It was my favorite winter outfit.

The students at the school wore skirts and blouses or sweaters. The clothes worn by women in outside jobs were especially ugly. Mary, our next door neighbor, worked at the ski factory and wore black quilted pants and coat. I had forgotten how pretty clothes could be until later when we made a trip to Moscow to the American Embassy. Several young American girls worked there, and to me they looked like angels in their pretty, colorful clothes. But clothes were not as important to us over there as they had been in the States. Among our friends, clothes had nothing to do with the true worth of a person. To this day I find myself giving less and less importance to clothes. I do remember being able to buy some corduroy which I made into a straight skirt and wore with sweaters. I had brought a white silk dress from home which did not seem to be appropriate wear in our surroundings so Lauri's cousin Lily, who was a seamstress, took it apart and made it into collars for me to wear with my sweaters.

In connection with sewing, I had a most embarrassing experience. I had taken sewing back in high school but never had sewn anything for a man. We'd been able once again to buy some rather heavy material out of which I decided to make a pair of workpants for Lauri. I doubt that I had a pattern but probably opened an old worn-out pair to use in cutting. I then proceeded to sew up all the long seams which were the easiest to start with. At that point, however, I was at an impasse: how to put in the pockets, the fly, etc. Finally, I asked my friend Edla, who was a tailor, to finish them. She took one look and exclaimed in disgust, "What lame brain would start a pair of pants by first sewing up the sideseams?" She might have guessed who had done it, but I don't recall confessing to it.

We had movies in Petrozavodsk—we called them the *kinos*. One evening during the summer of 1935 we saw *Les Misérables* with my schoolmate Inkeri. The film was supposedly American-made but it did not strike us as such. It was shown in a "summer theater"—a wooden hall built in a park. All that day we'd had sudden downpours of rain every hour or so. We got to the theater during one of the dry periods but it soon began to rain again and, we discovered, the roof leaked copiously. Several umbrellas went up. We hadn't brought one, but stayed to see the movie even though soggy wet from head to bottom.

Although in the States we had lived a simple country life, in Karelia we found conditions even more primitive with hard work and only the bare necessities, so to speak. But being young and imbued with the idea of building a workers' paradise, as it was called, we took all the difficulties in stride, more or less. And we had fun, real fun. We saw humor in situations that at other times in other places might have offended us. We had good friends with whom we were compatible, who felt and thought as we did. So, although I was homesick . . . desperately homesick for my father and my two brothers . . . it was a thing apart from my daily life. I was quite content with never a thought of going back: I only wished my father and brothers could have been there with me.

Youth is resilient—hopeful—optimistic. And we were young.

Dave and Lily Metsälä, and their children, Viola and Hugo, taken in Michigan before they went to Karelia.

Ducks and Dachas

L: Hunting has always been my favorite sport and so I asked around the ski factory and found several hunters. They were mostly Finns from Finland, though, and they did not seem to think that an American could be any good as a hunter. Finally one foreman decided that I could go along on the next duck hunt. I was thrilled. Having hunted ducks ever since I was big enough to hold a shotgun, I felt I could handle my end.

So one weekend five of us, (three Finns, a Karelian and I), took the ski factory motor boat, towing two small rowboats, and arrived in the late afternoon at a bay on Lake Onega where we camped overnight. In the morning we split up and took off in the row boats: three in one boat and two of us in the other. I was with a guy who was supposed to be a real hot shot so I started poling the boat. There were plenty of birds. After my hot shot missed some easy shots, I decided to be ready for the next one. When it flew up we both shot, and he picked up the bird satisfied that he now had the range. The next bird he missed and began cussing his gun. I asked if I could try so we changed places. A pair of mallards got up and I got them both. In about an hour I'd shot three more and it was time for lunch. The other three hunters were back in camp without a single bird. My partner was all smiles as he showed our birds and kidded them about their lousy shooting. He never mentioned how he had done! In fairness I must say that I had the best gun in the gang. It was a Remington pump, twelve-gauge, that I had brought from the states, one of the best duck guns I have ever owned. I was glad to have it.

We knew of others who had been recuited in the States to work in the mines in Siberia and been urged to bring guns for hunting with them. The area, they were told, teemed with game. When they got to Leningrad customs officials took their guns, promising to send them on later. "Later" never came. I was lucky; I got to keep my gun. Perhaps it depended on the individual customs official.

After lunch I decided to walk the shoreline and jump shoot. After I had seven or eight birds my ammo got low. Back in camp one of the men, Vilho Saarinen, started reloading shells for me. I kept hunting, and by evening we had twenty-five ducks, I got credit for all but one. From then on I was never left out when there was a hunt planned.

We did quite a bit of hunting, mostly for sport, but, with meat so scarce, it sure was a big help to our diet. We would usually hunt in pairs and divide our catch fifty-fifty no matter who shot them. In the fall it was mostly partridge and rabbit. The rabbits were actually European hares much larger than our Michigan snowshoes. When we got only one I would split it down the middle. There was always more meat in half a rabbit than Sylvi and I could eat for one meal. The partridge were like ours—if anything, smaller. Squirrels were like our grey squirrels. We did eat a couple but somehow we didn't like the idea, and I usually gave them to my partner.

There was also a bird about the size of a pheasant called *tetyorka* in Russian and *teeri* in Finnish.* It was very good eating, and we were allowed to shoot them spring and fall. In the spring they would gather in certain little openings or fields and perform their mating dances. We would post ourselves in blinds before daybreak and wait for them. In March it was often very cold. We had to sit perfectly still; they were wary birds. A scout would come first and check the area. If he was satisfied, the rest would follow. On one occasion a bird settled right on top of my blind about three feet above my head. I didn't dare move a muscle. When it finally flew to the ground to join the others, I was so cramped I could hardly raise my gun but I got him: a nice big rooster with beautiful, colorful feathers.

The *metso* or capercaillie was the king of birds. It was a large grouse

*According to the Finnish-English dictionary by Aino Wuolle it is a black grouse.

about the size of a wild turkey. They were not very plentiful, and we had to travel quite deep into the woods to find them. The spring hunt was the most fun.

It would be some time in April when snow was still on the ground that we would venture into the deep woods after work. By 11:00 P.M. we would get to a likely area, build a fire and relax until 2:00 A.M. Then we would start out walking silently and listening for the male metso's song. It was just a light tapping, as if you were tapping a matchbox with your fingernail. "Tap, tap." Then he would listen a minute or so. Then there would be three or four taps. Pause. Five or six taps. Pause.Then, as he grew more confident, he would increase the pace to maybe three seconds of very fast taps followed by a short rubbing or scraping noise as if you were rubbing the edge of the matchbox briskly with your fingernail back and forth. Then there would be total silence as the bird looked around. If he didn't hear or see anything out of the ordinary the ritual would start all over again.

Our strategy would be this: after hearing the so-called song, we would try to sneak up on him while he was making noise. During his scraping sound there would be time to take about three quick steps or leaps, trying, of course, to stay out of sight behind trees and then waiting motionless till he started up again. In this way we would try to get within range of his perch which would be on a tree limb about twenty or thirty feet in the air.

I remember one such hunt where I had to go across a clearing of twenty feet or so. I took my time studying the spot and figured I would get half way on my first move and clear it on the second. My calculations were correct but as I reached the center I stepped on a log hidden under the snow and my foot twisted into a bad position. The bird must have heard it too, because he just turned mute. I was miserable: head down, foot cocked unnaturally trying to stay perfectly still while those sharp little eyes and ears strained in the semi-darkness. It seemed like forever before I heard "tap" and a long time before "tap, tap." Finally he was fooled, and I was able to get to cover. From there on it was easy. Once I got in range, I waited till he was in the scraping stage before shooting. Had I missed then, I might have had another shot at him; the old-timers had told me that the bird can't hear a thing when he is making that scraping noise, so that was the time to shoot.

While rummaging at the ski factory warehouse one day, I found the kind of carbide lamp that straps on your forehead. This, I thought, would be ideal for spearing fish at night. I hunted around some more and found a can of carbide and then asked the warehouse keeper what they were used for. He didn't know. He said the lamp had been there a long time, and I could have it if there was something I could use it for. There sure was.

That fall when bird hunting started I told one of my hunting buddies what I had and suggested that we go hunting to a place about four kilometers from town. There was a small cabin there, right on the lakeshore, a sort of a community place that anybody could use. Hunting was as good there as anywhere else. My plan was to stay overnight at the cabin, fish at night and hunt during the day. I took along my homemade spear, hip boots and the carbide lamp.

It was evening when we got to the cabin. To our surprise there were already two Karelian men there who had built a fire outside and were boiling water for tea. They asked us to join them, and even though the cabin was small, invited us to stay. The cabin was about eight by ten feet with a very low ceiling, with a platform made of split logs that served as our bed. There was a stove built of rocks with no chimney that could be fired up until the rocks got hot, and then the coals and ashes were cleared out. When the smoke cleared, it was a comfortable heat source even in cold weather, as the rocks would stay hot for a long time.

We sat around the fire until about 10:00 o'clock. The Karelians were fishing, too, but not with spears. They had set out what were known as hoop nets, cone-shaped nets about six to ten feet in diameter, as well as gill nets. Any way of catching fish was legal. When it got dark, I put on my carbide lamp and my hip boots and went out to try my luck. It was a grassy shoreline, and I walked in about two feet of water so clear I could see quite a distance. The fish were spooky, but finally I was able to sneak up on a pike. After spearing it and tying it to my belt, I got a big burbot, an eel-like fish that wrapped itself around my arm when I raised it from the water. I took them both back to camp.

That got the others interested, and we fished till after midnight, spearing a few more. Early in the morning, we took off hunting while the Karelians went to check their nets. They'd had pretty good luck. We shot a few birds. Adding them to the fish it was a real nice catch.

One fall the ski factory director, Tuomainen, asked if I would take a friend of his, a Russian army officer, out duck hunting. I was willing, and so the following Sunday we took off with a small outboard to Solomon Bay, just the two of us. The boat belonged to the head bookkeeper at the ski factory. I had repaired the motor for him, so he told me to use it whenever I wanted to. It was about a three- or four-horsepower single cylinder, in pretty good shape. The boat reminded me of the kind we had on the St. Mary's River in Michigan in the twenties.

The shooting was good, and the officer was a sharp shooter. We had a fine time and, by late afternoon, a nice bag of birds, too. I suggested that we should get back home, but he kept saying, "Let's hunt some more," and so we did.

Finally I was getting worried, because I had told Sylvi that we would be back by dark, since we had plans for the evening. So I told the officer that my wife was waiting but he just brushed that off saying, "*Zhonka nye utka, nye letit kak utki*," ("a wife is not a duck, doesn't fly like a duck") so why worry? They definitely had a different attitude toward women over there. I finally persuaded him to leave because it was getting dark, and he very reluctantly agreed. He was quiet for a while on the way home, almost pouting, but then he began to discuss the hunt, and, by the time we got back, we were both in high spirits. He was very grateful to me for taking him and hoped someday we could do it again.

We made our own fine shot for hunting by melting lead and then pouring it into holes in blocks of wood to form wire the same diameter as the shot we wanted. Then we cut the wire into pieces the same length as the diameter. This we did with a cutter I had made for the purpose. It was like a paper cutter with an adjustable stop so the pieces were uniform in length. The next step was to round the pellets by putting them into a metal can about two and a half by five inches and shaking the can so the pellets would bounce around and wear into a round shape. I used to bolt the can to the eccentric on the power house steam engine for about a half hour; it would shake them back and forth till they came out smooth and round. I usually did this on a free day when the factory wasn't running so I could start and stop the steam engine while doing maintenance.

In the fall of 1935 we started to build the Finnish sled called a *potku kelkka* at the ski factory. It was very popular. We had one too, and often used it to go places like visiting Dave and Lily or into town. It had long steel runners like skates: two narrow blades ¼ inch by 1½ inches by eight feet long, with a chair up in front for a rider. The driver would stand in back with one foot on a runner, pushing and kicking with other. On a down hill he would ride with one foot on each runner. The handle bars were used for steering as well as pushing. The flexible steel blade allowed for sharp turns. The sled worked very well on the hard-packed snow of our streets in winter. This hard surface, good for sledding or skating, was known as *pääkallo keli* or "skull condition."

One evening after work, a Karelian fellow, Ronkanen, and I were going to the ski factory club house for some doings. The club house was about a half mile from the ski factory along the lakeshore, next to the ski factory garage. I was suppose to receive an award for some money-saving improvements I had made at the factory. We stopped at Ronkanen's place to get his *potku kelkka* to take into town. Before we left though, he wanted me to sample some of his homemade beer, called "*braug*," which he claimed was especially good. It was made from sugar, grain and raisins fermented under pressure. He did warn me that it was also pretty powerful stuff. So I tried some. It was sweet and didn't taste very good to me but we both had two big glasses. Then we left for the club with me driving the sled. We were going pretty fast down hill, maybe twenty or thirty miles an hour, when we met a bus coming up the hill. I steered close to the snowbank to avoid the bus. All of a sudden I found myself sliding on my stomach on the crusty snow with the handle bar in my hands but no sled! Ronkanen had made a somersault into the snow; the sled had come to a halt in a snowbank.

We were a bit banged up. Ronkanen had some blood on his nose, and my face was scratched from the hard crust on the snow. We looked over the damage and decided that we could steer the sled without the handle bar just by holding on to the uprights. Ronkanen wanted to drive; he wasn't going to depend on me anymore! So I sat in the sled, and he did pretty well until we got close to the club. There was a steeper area on the hill and a sharp turn at the bottom which we missed. Over the bank we went and right into a telephone pole. I was still sitting on the seat hugging the pole when Eino and Ben came from the garage across the road where they had been working overtime, to see what had happened. We were still determined to go to the club, but they took one look at us and sent us home in a hurry. Sylvi wasn't too harsh on me. When I looked in the mirror I could see why. My face was a real mess and it was just beginning to sting.

The ski factory had some property across Lake Onega from Petrozavodsk where workers could build summer cabins which the Russians call *dachas*. This area was known as *Pässinranta*, literally "goat's shore," and many of our friends had cabins there. During her summer vacation in 1935, which did not coincide with mine, Sylvi was able to spend five days at Heino's cabin with her friend Flossie, picking blueberries and sun bathing. But of course we wanted to build our own cabin.

The director wanted us to build on factory property, like all the others, but we wanted to be further away. We leased land from the government and got permission to build our *dacha* on a beautiful, rocky point about a half mile from the ski factory cabins. Not being on the factory property, our cabin could be built however we wanted while the factory cabins all had to be the same type of construction, and if you ever quit the factory you would have to move out. (It was possible to quit and find work elsewhere but few people did; the ski factory was a good place to work.)

We went together on the cabin with Lily and Dave and built it from logs. We picked a lot of them right there off the lakeshore. Dave knew how to hollow out one side of the log to a concave shape so it would fit snugly onto the one below. The corners were made in the Finnish style to lock them together. We worked weekends through the winter of 1935 and got the walls up. In the spring of 1936, we had a motor boat pulling a scow to bring in lumber which we'd been able to buy from a sawmill near the ski factory. We used the boards for window frames, doors, and flooring. There was no roofing material available, so Dave suggested that we make a board roof. The boards were about ¾ inch by 8 inches wide. We planed grooves along each edge about ½ inch wide and ¼ inch deep about ¾ inches from the side of the board and nailed the boards on top of the stringers as close together as possible. Then we nailed four-inch-wide boards over each seam. This way, if some water seeped in under the four-inch boards, it would drain off in the grooves and run down the slope. I don't remember having any leaks from this roof. Years later I saw some roofs like ours on old buildings in Finland.

By summer of 1936 we were able to use the cabin. We really enjoyed spending summer weekends out there with friends. It was on one of these weekends that we built the outhouse. We had four couples out that day, and when it came time to cut out the seat we looked at all the women, and decided that Inki Kent had the biggest bottom. We therefore asked her to sit on the seat so we could draw a line around her, figuring if it was big enough for her, the rest of us would be happy with it. Inki protested at first but, good sport that she was, she went along with the plan, and we had a hilarious time. All our friends contributed in some way to the cabin but Inki's share was the most fun.

Not far from our cabin lived a Karelian family by the name of Kanerva. They had a sauna built on a rocky point on the shore of Lake Onega. We were allowed to use the sauna in return for food items, vodka and such goodies. Cutting wood for the sauna each time we used it was a must. Akulina, the lady of the house, made sure we did not fail at this. She was a husky woman who ruled her family with an iron fist. Her husband, Alexander, was afraid of her and with good reason. I remember one evening when we had arrived at our cabin with our friends Eino and Sylvi Dahlstrom. Alexander came over to greet us as usual. He was down in the dumps, but, after a few drinks, he perked up and was soon singing away in a high-pitched monotone, taking a few dance steps as he sang. Just as we were beginning to enjoy his song and dance act, Akulina arrived screaming and yelling at him for drinking when there was so much work to be done. He tried to placate her, but she grabbed him by the ear and started towing him home. Now he was the one who was screaming and yelling. As far as we could hear them, he was complaining about how much it hurt and begging her to let go of his ear. To us it was funny, but to Alexander it was far from it.

One Saturday or Sunday some friends of Dave and Lily's, Vilho and Terttu, were visiting with us at the cabin. Seeing Dave and Lily coming down the path, Terttu turned to her husband and said, "Let's hide and surprise them." Our ceiling rafters were covered with sheets of plywood, some of them nailed down but some still loose. We told them to hide up there, and they quickly scrambled up. Vilho sat securely on nailed boards but Terttu, unfortunately, chose to perch on a loose piece. Just as Dave opened the cabin door, the piece of plywood gave way and crashed to the floor, leaving her, with her dress caught under her armpits, clinging desperately to a crossbeam. To say that Dave and Lily were surprised is to understate the case. We were all speechless for several moments until Vilho recovered sufficiently to come and help her down.

Realizing that she wasn't hurt, only a bit embarrassed, I got my wits about me and made us a drink to relax. Then it hit us; the more we discussed it the funnier it got.

"Biggest and best surprise I ever had," Dave declared.

We were doing quite well at this time and had hired an elderly lady, a Mrs. Mäntynen, to do our laundry while Sylvi was in school. Mrs. M. spent the summer in Pässinranta and did our washing there so we would pick it up when we were at our cabin on weekends. One day we had left a couple of suitcases of freshly laundered clothes in our cabin while visiting friends—most of our summer clothes, in fact. Before we returned, someone broke into the cabin and stole them.

We could tell immediately when we came back that they had broken in. We had American-style windows on the cabin which the robbers couldn't open. Karelian windows opened out, French style, while ours slid up. The frustrated thieves had taken off the whole frame!

What a horrible feeling. We knew we couldn't replace the clothes.

Lauri and Sylvi at their *dacha*.

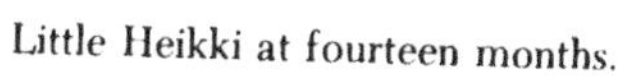

Little Heikki at fourteen months.

Sylvi Dahlstrom and baby Helen.

Eino Dahlstrom.

I went to town and reported the theft to the authorities, but they did not seem concerned. After a big hassle I was able to get a couple of bloodhounds and we tried to track the thieves. We found some of the stuff that they had thrown away. We must have been close to them but we didn't catch them and were left without a large part of our wardrobe.

More Action, Fewer Words

L: The ski factory was named after Edward Gylling, the Chairman of the Karelian Executive Committee and the top man in Karelia. He would often walk in, all by himself, take a look around and stop to talk to some of the workers. Several times he asked me questions about the operation and how I felt. He never made any pretense of being better than anyone else. I liked him, and so did everyone I knew. We looked up to him. But in the fall of 1935 he was called to Moscow. We all wondered why he had to go. People were always being sent to different places, and, of course, we wondered about it, but we had learned that it was safer not to ask too many questions. We never saw Gylling in Karelia again, and his place was taken by an arrogant bureaucrat who was so paranoid that he had two fully armed bodyguards protecting him whenever he came to the ski factory.

One day we heard that a group of Russian scientists who had spent a year in the arctic were going to visit the ski factory. This created a lot of excitement. We had been reading in the newspapers about this group and the tests they had been making. Before their arrival the management went all out to prepare a reception for the Soviet heroes, even building a special platform for the elite to speak from, outdoors on the ski factory grounds.

The day they came I was having trouble with an overheated bearing on one of the ski-bottom planers. I decided to change the bearing during the festivities, so as soon as everyone was told to gather around the platform, I went to work.

It so happened that the leader of this scientific group, one Papanin, had stated that he wanted to see the factory in operation and never mind the speeches. By-passing the crowd around the platform, he headed straight into the factory and soon came upon me trying to fix the machine. He wanted to know what I was doing, and I explained as best I could. He was very pleased. He ended up praising me in front of everyone, telling them this was the way to keep production going.

"*Bolshe dyela, menshe slova,*" he said, which is an old Russian proverb meaning "more action, fewer words."

Good work was always appreciated at the ski factory, and this was encouraging to all of us who worked there. Most of us worked hard and were proud of what we accomplished. Men and women were treated fairly equally, it seems to me. A woman could go to work in the factory, or anywhere, and get the same pay as a man if she could cut the mustard.

There was one young Karelian woman in her early twenties working in the ski factory lumber yard. She was built like a wrestler, a powerful Katrinka, and she could outdo most men but was apprehensive about what the men would do if she earned more than they did. She went to the factory director and asked him if it was permissible for her to do better than the men. Since it was piecework it was easy to see how much each person produced. The director told her to do as much as she could and it would be to her credit. From then on she was a Soviet hero. They started giving her bonuses, and there were pictures of her in the newspapers as an example to others.

There were several Finnish-language newspapers in Petrozavodsk at that time. I remember one of these papers printed a picture of strikers parading in front of a Detroit automobile plant, probably some time in 1936. The paper didn't call it a strike though; they referred to it as a "hunger march" and told what a horrible time the workers in the United States were having. One of the ski factory foremen, a Russian, looked at this picture and said to me, "They don't look so hungry. See how many are overweight, and look how well dressed they are."

I made no comment knowing that it was best to keep my mouth shut. Everybody was cautious. You didn't brag. You didn't say anything that you thought could possibly be used against you, and to praise anything about a capitalist country was certainly in that category. You could be called a counter-revolutionary and people had been arrested for that.

The foreman told me a little about his childhood. He had worked in a flour mill that his father had built to grind grain for their village. After the revolution they lost everything. His father was called a *kulak*, and the government took over the mill and also their horse and cow. All they had left was the clothes on their backs. They were punished for being too ambitious.

It seemed that many of these so-called *kulaks* were just small farmers with a couple of cows who worked harder and got a little wealthier than their neighbors. My friend remembered that his father wouldn't let him go to dances* with the other young people because he always had to work.

His story reminded me of Sylvi's father, Frank Kuusisto, who owned a small farm and store on Sugar Island. He used to joke with friends that, strictly speaking, he was really a *kulak*. They would laugh about it, but I wondered what would have happened if the revolution had come to the United States. I could see that if he had been living in Russia the same way he lived in the States, he surely would have been called a *kulak* and lost everything.

It was also some time in 1936 that Sylvi came home from school in tears. She had been told that she couldn't go to school any more because we weren't Russian citizens and didn't have a Russian passport. She was preparing to teach Finnish and English and for that, she was told, she would need a Russian passport. We wondered what we should do.

Had this happened in 1937, we probably wouldn't have done it, but in 1936 things were going well for us, and Sylvi was looking forward to teaching. We went ahead and applied for a Russian passport not realizing that by doing this, we were becoming Russian citizens and thereby losing our American citizenship. I remember how shocked I was when they asked for my American passport, "Why should I give you this?" I wondered, but I did. It wasn't long before we realized what a big mistake that had been.

I only remember voting once in Karelia. When they had an election, everyone had to vote. People went from barracks to barracks opening every door to tell everyone that they must go and vote—right now. I went to the ski factory office and was given a ballot to mark but there was only one name on it, the name of the person chosen by the Party to

---

*Village dances were held on wooden bridges at that time, since they were the only places of any size with a smooth surface.

represent our district. The rest of us had no choice, but we were all expected to come out and ratify the Party's choice. It was such a farce. It really made us wonder what kind of a deal we had gotten into.

Around this time the ski factory restaurant burned to the ground leaving only a few walls standing and the brick chimney. We were allowed to scavenge some boards from the ruins for firewood and there must have been at least twenty of us out there, pulling up boards and carting them home, when suddenly the wall next to the chimney collapsed bringing the chimney down with it. One man happened to be under it; he was buried in the rubble. It took us about half an hour to reach him but we were too late. He was dead. That was the end of the free firewood. The fire department fenced it off.

Accidents also were becoming more frequent at the factory, as they were trying to speed up production and doing a lot of piecework. Many of the machines had poor safety guards. Some, in fact, had no safety guards at all, because the operators had removed them in order to work faster. I was told to put on more guards and replace those that had been taken off. Of course some of the operators were unhappy with this, but after a few weeks they got used to working with the guards, and the complaints decreased.

One machine presented a problem. There was no way to set up an ordinary guard. I designed and set up a spring that would clip you on the fingers if you pushed your hands too close to the cutters. Eager to see how it worked, I kept my eye on the girl who operated it the first day the device was on. I saw her fingers getting closer and closer to the cutter; then it sprang. She jerked her hand back and her face turned white. Quite shaken, she examined her fingers and found them all intact. Then, turning red, she raced for the mechanic's office screaming that someone had put something on her machine that scared her half to death. By then, I was in the office too, trying to keep a straight face. It took a lot of explaining to convince her that the spring was for her own good, but it worked so well we never had any more cut fingers from that particular machine.

Things were looking up at that time. Our standard of living was improving noticeably. New stores were being built, and consumer goods began to appear on the shelves. If a person had the money and time to stand in line, luxury items, such as a radio, or make-up, were available. In the fall of 1936, Sylvi began teaching Finnish language and literature. She was earning about 1,000 rubles a month—twice what I usually made with overtime, and four times the salary of the average worker. Back in the States she had earned $90 a month teaching, which was about the same wage a Ford factory worker made. I felt that the Soviets were on the right track in paying their teachers so well.

I believe it was in the summer of 1936 that the government offered glider instruction to those who were interested at a field near town, so we got a group of eight together to learn the ABCs of gliding. Our instructor was a young air force officer who taught some theory of flying and also gave us some field experience.

We would set up the glider anchored to the ground with a steel cable and a release hook. The instructor would hold on to the tip of the wing and tell the learner just how to adjust the controls. Meanwhile the rest of us would lay out a hundred foot rubber cable attached to the front of the glider. The instructor would then tell us how far to stretch out this rubber cable, say fifty steps or so. It would stretch double its length or more if fully extended. So the guy in the lead would count as we pulled it fifty steps and then stopped. Then the person in the glider was told to pull the release lever. The cable would jerk the glider about fifty to sixty feet in the air and the student would glide back to the ground. The perfect glide had to be smooth with wings level—a nice long ride and good landing.

I was the last one to take a ride, confident as usual, and the rest of them knew it so they decided to give me a real thrill. They counted fifty steps, but actually took seventy-five or more. The instructor didn't notice; he was too busy getting me started. When I released the glider I shot high up in the air and almost stalled before leveling off. Then I dove for the ground, pulled back too much, went up and then down again before managing to level off for the glide. I must have been a sight. Some of the others were doubled up with laughter. I was just happy the glider didn't get wrecked.

The hardest part for me was the direction control. I had a hard time getting over my sled riding as a kid. On a sled, when you pushed the bar with your left foot you went to the right. On the glider, it is just the opposite. We had about ten lessons and it was a lot of fun—something I have fond memories of—but then the lessons were suddenly stopped with no explanation why.

A Russian hunter friend had wanted for a long time to buy my Remington shotgun or trade me for his double barrel shotgun. I didn't want to sell, but he finally wore me down. The price was good so I gave in, but first I had to go to the border guards for permission. When I got there I was directed to an office where a man sat in full uniform with medals and the works plus a long sword at his side. Very impressive. I explained what I wanted. "Have you sold anything at the *tori*?" he wanted to know.

The tori in Petrozavodsk was what we would call a flea market where people sold used items they didn't want. It was evidently legal since it was right out in the open. I told him my wife had sold a pair of shoes and a party dress. Why did he care, I wondered.

He gazed at me for a while and then abruptly barked, "You already sold that gun!" He claimed, loudly, that I had sold the gun and then come for the permit, emphasizing his words by drawing his sword almost out of its scabbard and slamming it back in. It scared the hell out of me. He continued to do this, accusing me of selling other things illegally, always punctuating his words with the banging of his sword. Finally I was allowed to go home. The permit was never mentioned, and I was not about to bring it up again. When I told my friend I wasn't going to sell the gun because I couldn't get permission he said, "Oh you don't need permission." I probably could have gotten away with selling it without a permit, but I wanted to be up front and do things properly. It was far too easy to get in trouble over there, and I didn't want to take a chance.

Four of us at the ski factory had "boat fever." We kept asking if anyone knew of a boat engine we could buy. Finally we found an Opal four-cylinder that was so bad it had to be rebuilt. It was cheap enough, and we bought it and decided to cut it in half to make two two-cylinder engines. We had to make new piston rings, new valves, new flywheel, new timing gears; the cylinder walls had to be honed, and lots more. The pistons and flywheel we had to have cast in the Onegzavod Foundry. The honing and grinding was done at Karelian Auto. (The Karelian auto machine shop had mostly American-made machinery brought by Finnish-Americans to repair autos and trucks.)

Keijo Frilund and I built up one half of the engine. The other was made by Arne Tuomainen and another American Finn whose name I can't remember. We got our engine finished first by working evenings. I had bet the others a bottle of whiskey that it would start right off when I had it together, so one evening we gathered together at the shop to test it out. Sure enough, it started, although it sounded like a four-cycle four-cylinder engine running on just two cylinders. We celebrated so much that night that it cost them two bottles of whiskey, plus headaches the following morning.

The other two fellows got their boat built, working evenings at the ski factory and using factory equipment. They got to use the boat some, and it worked well. We didn't get ours built at all. Things were changing. Everything was tightening up, and this kind of private endeavor was discouraged.

The director of the ski factory, Elias Tuomainen, had been given a car for his own use, one of the first Ford V8s ever made. A man from Drummond Island, Michigan, had brought the car to Karelia. He was compensated for it in rubles at the rate of two rubles per dollar—a very unrealistic rate considering that white bread sold for 4.40 rubles a kilo and was ten cents a loaf in the United States, and Sylvi paid 14 rubles for a small padlock that would have been fifty or sixty cents at home.

Eino Dahlstrom, our good friend from Canada, worked as a mechanic at the ski factory garage. He was given the job of chauffering the director in the Ford. This was quite an honor and a very responsible job. One night on an icy road he rolled the car over. The body was banged up some, but the worst of it was that the transmission housing was cracked all the way around. The accident created quite a stir in town, and we were afraid Eino might even land in jail, but the director said if we could get it to run in a couple of days it would take some of the heat off.

At that time nobody would arc weld cast iron. We just had steel rod to weld with but that was our only hope. We bolted it together and put it in a forge at the blacksmith shop until it was beginning to glow. Then I started to weld about an inch at a time with the others peening it right after. We kept this up until late at night and covered it up with hot coals to let it cool slowly.

The next day Eino and Ben, another Canadian, worked at assembling the transmission while some others hammered the body into shape. By the end of the day, Eino had the car parked in front of the office. It ran okay and the heat was off.

Gasoline was in short supply and very expensive. Some of the logging trucks were converted to run on gas extracted from wood. These trucks used gasoline only for starting and warming up the motor; then they switched to wood gas or methanol. On the outside of the truck next to the fender was the firebox that the wood was burned in. Then there were two filtering tanks mounted behind the cab that coverted the smoke to gas that was piped directly into the motor. In this way the distilling process was unnecessary.

The drawbacks of these trucks were that they were less efficient, having about thirty percent less power, and they smelled bad, especially when the motor was shut off. This was because the fire would still be burning and the smoke would not be converted into gas. We usually ran these trucks all day and didn't put the fire out until evening.

The ski factory lumber yard had no tractor to haul lumber and logs around, and there wasn't room for a truck. The management asked for suggestions, and the boys from the garage suggested shortening an old model A truck and making it into a tractor. Eino Dahlstrom, Benny Laine and I took it on a contract to build. I was included to do the welding and cutting. This was a fun job for all of us. We were doing something we had never seen done, and it was quite a challenge. We would start working on it by 7:00 o'clock in the evening and work until midnight every night.

We had a half liter bottle of vodka that we called "bear juice" because there was a picture of a bear on the bottle. Several times during the evening someone would yell "bear juice" and we would stop work for a drink and a short conference. (Since we had no drawings for this project it was sometimes necessary to stop and discuss the problems we ran into.)

The job turned out to be one of the best money makers for us and also for the factory. The thing could turn on a dime, so to speak. The management was very pleased with their new tractor and we were praised for the good work. That's when Eino and I got the good idea to ask for a few days off to go to Leningrad for some relaxation. Permission granted.

Eino and Sylvi Dahlstrom, Sylvi and I, took off for Leningrad by train. We were in a festive mood. Money was plentiful, so we ate and drank the best that was available and checked into a beautiful old hotel—I think it was called the Metropole. What luxury! We had four rooms with a tub bath, a piano, overstuffed sofas and chairs and gilded tables. Everything was just grand.

The first day we walked a lot. In the evening, tired, we decided to use a taxi. From then on it was taxis, nightclubs, restaurants—nothing but the best. The only shopping we did was a pair of galoshes for Eino and a hat for me.

After three days and nights we were ready to go back and presented ourselves at the hotel desk to check out and collect our passports. The rule was that whenever you went anywhere away from your home you had to register with the police. Hotel management routinely took the passports of their guests and showed the police who was staying there. If the police wanted to question you, they simply took your passport knowing you couldn't go anywhere without it and would soon come to retrieve it.*

Eino, Sylvi and I received our passports with no problem but Sylvi Dahlstrom's, we were told, had been taken by the NKVD, the secret police, today known as the KGB. They gave us the address to go and get it.

With only a few hours until train time, the four of us took a taxi to the big, grey brick building. Eino and Sylvi Dahlstrom went in; we stayed in the taxi trying to figure out why we were being detained. For over an hour we sat there worrying about what was going on and wondering if we would miss our train. All kinds of thoughts went through our heads but we kept telling each other that of course it would all be straightened out. What's wrong with going on a trip?

Finally they came out and we dashed to the station. After we got our tickets they told us what had transpired with the police. First, the NKVD had wanted to know why we were in Leningrad since we were not on vacation. How did we get time off? What had we been doing? Did we buy anything? Meet with any friends? They couldn't see why we should be running around having fun instead of working. Apparently, the Dahlstroms' answers were satisfactory; we all returned to Petrozavodsk without any more trouble, but it was a rude ending to a fun weekend.

---

*After 1932, all citizens except peasants had to carry an internal passport. It didn't matter whether peasants had one since they weren't allowed to travel anywhere anyway. (Kort 183)

"We Like That Little One"

S: It was a great thrill for us in Karelia to get letters from America. Several people wrote to us—my father, brother Andrew, and Lauri's mother, Evi, mostly. My close friend from Sugar Island, Impi Maki, wrote quite often. She and Andrew would put little things into letters. Most of them would not reach me. In a letter I wrote her in March 1935, I lamented, "I haven't received a thing you've sent me. I just cried over that collar . . . I know it was sweet . . . somebody has it, I know. I wish you would send more little things in letters."

Andrew would put in sticks of gum and handkerchiefs; I did receive a few of those. Lauri's sister Irja wrote once to announce her coming marriage and once to announce the birth of her first baby, a boy named Lauri Andrew who died in infancy.

Bureaucrats and red tape were plentiful while we were in Karelia. During the summer of 1935 we decided to have our pictures taken. This took all summer. It was not at all what we'd been used to in the States. The very first thing one did was pay. We paid for six pictures. Then we sat for them and were told when to come for them. I did. The young lady in charge sorted through a stack of pictures asking, "Is this it?" with each one. Our pictures were not there. She just said, "Come again." I did. She spoke Russian; I could understand her, but she did not understand my Finnish and finally found someone who could translate. I asked her as sharply as I dared how many times one had to come and sit before a picture could be made. She assured me one more time would do it. We did eventually get our pictures, although I can't recall how many times we had to go to the studio.

During the summer of 1935 Lauri and I went to visit my Uncle Frank in Solomanni, about twenty miles by bus. There was a sawmill there where Uncle Frank worked filing saws. My aunt, his first wife, had died after they moved to Karelia, and Uncle had married a Karelian woman. She was a very gentle soul and treated us well. Uncle's teenage son Arvo by his first wife was living with them.

Uncle Frank and his family lived in a small, old Karelian house and kept a few animals. One of their pigs had been fattened for slaughter, and they asked Lauri to butcher it for them. Uncle's wife had become quite attached to the porker and could not bear the thought of its being hurt. Lauri assured her that when he hit the animal it would drop dead without a sound, but later she insisted she'd heard it squeal. We had a big meal that day consisting of a soup made of potatoes and, as a second course, potatoes with just a bit of meat. We were also given a piece of the pig to take home with us. Later Lauri had a chance to slaughter a pig for someone at the ski factory and again came home with a piece of pork for his labor.

Uncle Frank had always treated me like a child, and on this visit he did it again, much to my embarrassment. He and Lauri stayed up late after his wife and I had gone to bed. After a long time I awoke and, finding Lauri still missing, got up to see what was going on. There they sat at the kitchen table with a bottle of vodka between them. When Uncle saw me, he told me to go right back to bed and not bother them. I didn't dare protest.

Later I heard the story of their vodka drinking. Lauri had brought one bottle along with him, and they had sat drinking and talking about old times back in the States until, to their surprise, the bottle was empty. Uncle Frank then went to retrieve a bottle he had stashed away outdoors. It was, as it happened, forty degrees below zero Celsius that night and the vodka had actually frozen to slush. After a few minutes in the warm house, however, it cleared up and they resumed their drinking.

There was a cemetery not far from the ski factory, and I will never forget seeing and hearing my first Russian funeral. The mourners were most articulate; the weeping and wailing could be heard for quite a distance. It was mostly the women. They would throw themselves on the grave and carry on. I had never heard grief so openly voiced, and it struck me as being exaggerated and forced. Russians were apt to be more outgoing than the stoic Finns; it was normal with them. The well-known funeral march was generally played at funerals and it was very moving.

Ordinarily, I stayed at home with my schoolwork when Lauri went to the club for his band practice sessions, but now and then I would tag along with my books and papers and study in some side room. Although I'd be alone in the room, I felt compelled to stand whenever the band played the "Internationale." This song was the national anthem of the Soviet Union at the time. It was sung by workers all over the world. I'd heard it many times as a child. The Finnish people on Sugar Island sang a Finnish version of it at all their social gatherings, and it was a solemn moment fraught with deep meaning. We always stood up while singing it. I especially remember one line: "*Huomis päivänä kansat on veljet keskenään,*" (Tomorrow all nations will be brothers together). As a little child I thought it meant that tomorrow my brothers would be alone together! But the feeling of solemnity as well as exaltation associated with the "Internationale" had stayed with me, and I always had to stand whenever I heard it played. Childhood memories and feelings die hard.

Lauri worked at the ski factory throughout our stay in Petrozavodsk. He had always been a good, conscientious worker from the time he was a boy, and he continued to do his best at the ski factory. He was often rewarded for his efforts with bonuses, praise at meetings, and by having his picture in the paper. He was a *Stahanovilainen* (the Finnish term) or *Stakhanovist* (in Russian). Stakhanov was a coal miner somewhere in the south of Russia who consistently exceeded the daily norm set for the miners, sometimes even doubling the average output per man, or so we were told. He was highly praised in the newspapers, called a hero of the Soviet Union, and made an example for others to follow. The best workers, therefore, in other areas and lines of work were given the name *Stakhanovist*, in his honor. Often it was difficult to see how the work could be assessed or graded, but somehow this was done and the awards passed out. It was fine for workers who had no problem getting out a lot of work, but there were workers, too, who tried just as hard but could not accomplish as much for one reason or another. For them the *Stakhanovist* label was perhaps discouraging.

The Karelian Pedagogical Institute, which I attended, was a two-year school. During my second year, 1935-1936, we did our practice teaching at the secondary school in Petrozavodsk. Our whole class would go over to the school, and, while one of us would take over in the regular teacher's place, the rest of the class would observe. I remember my turn very well. While waiting in the hallway to enter the classroom, I began to yawn, and yawn and yawn! My classmate, Sampsa, told me that yawning was a sign of nervousness, and that I was gasping for oxygen. However, my lesson went very well. One of the things that had been stressed to us was that the pupils should be left with an interest in the next lesson. I was lucky: the children followed me out of the room, asking questions about the next day's lesson. Later, the regular teacher told me I had done a good job, and the kids had said, "We really like that little one."

The class was in literature, and the subject that day was Charles Dickens' *Oliver Twist*, which the children were studying in a Finnish translation. One of the children read from the book, and we discussed it. I recall that when she read, "*ottakaa varas kiinni*" which was the Finnish version of "stop thief," it seemed to me that the Finnish was much more formal and stiff than English. At that time most Finnish seemed to me to be just that, but, of course, once I learned to speak it more fluently, I found it wasn't always so.

In June 1936 our studies at the Institute were over. Our class made a trip to Leningrad to celebrate. I do not recall much of what we did—saw the sights, the palaces, and the parks. I do remember being glad to be back home. This was the August that we received word of my brother Andrew's death from what was known as "galloping tuberculosis." He had become ill in May and died in early June. Lauri's mother, Evi, was the one who first wrote about it. Her letter came a couple of months after he had died, and she had assumed that my father had already let us know. It was an awful blow to me. My father wrote later saying he had been afraid to tell me knowing what a shock it would be to me. Andrew and I had been very close, and his death was heartbreaking for me. I wrote to my father asking him to come to us in Karelia, but he wrote back that he was too ill to make any such plans. He was suffering from silicosis, miners' tuberculosis. I hadn't realized he was sick. He died a few months later in February of 1937. My younger brother Arvo, who had also contracted tuberculosis, entered a sanitarium where he remained for four years. He and I had little contact with each other during those years.

After graduating from the Institute in June, I waited to be assigned to a teaching job. This was a nerve wracking time for all the graduates, as we wondered where we would be sent. Many of us, at least those with families in Petrozavodsk, dreaded being sent to some small, far-away village. I was assigned to the secondary school in Petrozavodsk, called the *Suomalainen Keski Koulu* (Finnish Middle School), where I had done my practice teaching, to teach Finnish language and literature to sixth, seventh and eighth graders.

During the year that I taught at the secondary school, fall 1936 to summer 1937, I also held lectures on Finnish literature for the students at the Finnish Dramatic Theater. These students were budding actors and actresses. I did not enjoy the job. Acting being what it is, many of the students were very mindful of their looks and facial expressions, to the point where some of them spent most of the lecture time gazing at themselves in hand mirrors and, no doubt, dreaming of the time when they would be famous on stage. This proved to be very disconcerting to me.

My close friend Inkeri Letonmaki had also been assigned to teach at the secondary school, and she and I usually walked to school together. Inkeri's family had a small house all to themselves, and it was on my way to school. Her father, Lauri Letonmaki, worked for the Finnish-language newspaper *Punainen Karjala* (*Red Karelia*).* In the spring of 1937 he was divested of his party membership. This was a sign that he was in some kind of trouble. One morning when I stopped to pick up Inkeri she told me she would not be going to school that day. Her father, despondent over losing his party membership and fearful, no doubt, of what lay ahead, had hanged himself during the night. It was a bad time for Inkeri, her older sister, and her mother. When I visited her during the days to come, I often found her mother playing solitaire (patience). A doctor had recommended it to her to save her from a nervous breakdown.

Our class from the Institute was able to teach only one year, 1936-37. After that the government stopped the teaching of Finnish in the schools. Finnish newspapers were discontinued; we were not even supposed to speak Finnish in public. This was in line with Stalin's paranoia; he felt that the Finns were trying to make Karelia into a Finnish republic.**

In the fall of 1937, I was given a job teaching in an all-Russian sec-

---

*Lauri Letonmaki, editor of political works, had been Minister of Justice in Finland's 1918 revolutionary government. (Tuominen 296).

**On July 25, 1937, Edvard Gylling, his wife, and Kustaa Rovio were arrested in Moscow. Most of the members of the Karelian government were also arrested, and the party secretaryship was assumed by a man named Kuprianov, who reportedly said at his inauguration, "I won't sleep peacefully a single night until the last Finn has been banished from Petrozavodsk." (Tuominen 299).

ondary school. I could not make a go of it. The pupils knew no English, and my knowledge of the Russian language was not good enough. My discipline was terrible. I had several young lads in the class who continually disrupted the whole class. I repeatedly asked the principal to come and oversee my lessons and to help me with discipline, but he never would enter my classroom. I thought it was probably his first job as principal, and he was just as afraid of the kids as I was. On the other hand, perhaps he did not want me teaching there since I was a foreigner. A school friend of mine, Selma Anderson, who also had been teaching at the secondary school when the Finnish language was banned, was sent to teach English in a Russian Technicum in Petrozavodsk. She soon lost this job because she was a "foreigner," and "foreigners" were not allowed to teach in Russian schools at this time. In my case, the situation became so difficult that I finally just stayed home, and no one ever came around to ask why I didn't come back.

That same fall an NKVD man and his wife came to live in our barracks at 50 Bolotnaya Ulitsa. I don't know how we knew he was of their ranks, but, somehow, we all did. Perhaps this couple was put there to keep an eye on the Finns. The wife was quite friendly, but one look from the man's gimlet eyes made cold chills run up and down one's spine and killed any urge for a closer relationship with them.

The winter of 1937-38 was a very severe one in Karelia, the hardest we had seen. That was the winter Lauri made me a pair of *tallukkaat*—a kind of soft shoe. We used my old snowsuit that we'd brought with us from the states which was getting worn. He made a pattern, cut out as many pieces as he could of each part of the pattern, and then sewed them together. For the soles, he used some kind of tough, rubbery belting he found at the factory. The *tallukkaat* proved to be comfortable, very warm and even cute.

This was the winter we made regular use of the woolen comforter we had brought with us; other winters we had needed it only occasionally. This was also the winter the ski factory band boys had to use *pirtua* (pure alcohol) in their horns to keep them from freezing. Naturally, the players had to have firewater of some sort in themselves, too, to keep warm.

Since the Soviet Union was an atheistic country we did not celebrate Christmas as such, but we did celebrate the New Year. We had a tree and a character called Father Frost. In December of 1937 we made plans for a New Year's party. Since our home was only one room, we could not have many guests. We had asked cousin Lily and Dave, our close friends Eino and Sylvi, and also Mary and Eino who lived behind the wall from us. We wanted Benny and Miriam with us, but they had a small baby and could not go out because of her.

Although Lily and Dave had separated earlier, they were ashamed to admit this to us, and would visit us, and have us over, as if nothing had happened. They would appear at our home together, and, when we visited at their home, there was Dave. We learned of their separation much later. They both came to the New Year's party.

We planned a midnight supper with as much on the table as our purse could stand. The big thing was the tree with homemade decorations—that was great fun. As we prepared for the party we wondered what 1938 would bring.

Earlier in the fall we had become acquainted with a couple named Grandell from Detroit. Toivo Grandell worked for Karelian Auto. We liked them both immediately and told them about our party preparations. A few weeks before New Year's, he was arrested. We wondered what to do about inviting his wife. The other women coming felt that it would not do, but I happened to meet her downtown one day and told her we would like to have her if she felt like coming. She did not, probably thinking that she might spoil the party for the rest of us.

It was a subdued little group that met that night to celebrate the New Year, and had we known what terror this particular year—1938—would bring, I am sure there would have been no celebrating at all.

Toivo Grandell's arrest was most disturbing. What could he have done? Would he be released?

All of us felt the frustration of not being able to say what we thought for fear of being considered disloyal. We thought the official attitude toward Stalin—giving him credit and thanking him for any and every good thing—was ridiculous, but we would never have dared to say so in public. We were all afraid.

Someone told a little story, with a kind of wry humor that seems typically Russian, that neatly illustrated the extent of our fears. It was about a woman who went fishing with some friends and caught only a very tiny fish. This she held up with obvious disdain and said sarcastically, "Thanks to Stalin." Someone reported her, as the story went, and she ended up in jail.

How Can They All Be Guilty?

L: For the first couple of years that we were in Karelia, the whole country was on a six-day week: five days of work at seven hours a day, and the sixth was a day of rest. Then the Supreme Soviet decided to change to a seven-day week and have six eight-hour work days with the seventh day off. People on salaries would get the same weekly pay as before; those on piece work would have their pay adjusted so they wouldn't make any more than they did before. It was a losing proposition for all workers.

To make this change legal, it had to be approved by all of the workers. The government printed a pamphlet describing the changes for people to read, and then held outdoor meetings at all of the factories. Not only were the new working hours introduced at this meeting, but some new rules as well. For instance, anyone who was late to work would be fined ten percent of his or her weekly pay for the first offense. The second lateness would result in a three-month jail sentence plus a twenty percent fine. What made this even worse was the fact that there were no alarm clocks to be had in the stores.

At the ski factory meeting we were told how many more fighter planes and jumbo carriers the state would be able to acquire with the money saved by these changes. Defense of the Motherland was important. Many other things were mentioned too. I did not hear a single voice protesting during the meeting. It was only in small groups afterward that people dared to complain. There was always the fear that someone would report you. It seemed impossible to those of us who had lived in a free society that such things could happen, but they did.

Instead of complaining, we all applauded whenever we were asked to approve a change. I especially remember how Ronkanen, who was often late to work, applauded so vigorously that afterward, back in the shop, one of the Karelians told the whole gang of us that Ronkanen had just applauded a jail sentence for himself! We all had a good laugh at Ronkanen's expense and sure enough, he did get a jail sentence later. I was fortunate; we had an alarm clock, brought from the states, so I was never late.

There was one time though, when that alarm clock didn't help me. The ski factory had a boat with a ten to twelve-horsepower motor. It was made in the Soviet Union and not very dependable, but I had occasion to use it every now and then to go to the cabin at Pässinranta or to go hunting or fishing. Since I took care of it, I didn't have to get anyone's permission to use it.

One beautiful summer evening after work several of us—a Karelian fellow from the power house, the Dahlstroms, Sylvi, and I—decided to make a quick trip to the cottage. On our way we stopped at a small store across the bay to see if they had anything we could use. (We often checked the different stores around, for what they might have.) To our surprise there was a big supply of one hundred-gram bottles of vodka, about the size available on airlines. They were sealed with paper stoppers, and, once opened, the contents had to be emptied. We bought about three-dozen bottles and set them in a couple of rows on the railings on the side of the boat. As we were riding we each had a bottle on which we sipped, then another, and another . . . by the time we got to the cabin, we didn't have a care in the world.

When it came time to go back into town, the motor wouldn't start. I did everything I could think of, but all it would do was sputter a little and quit. We were really worried. It was already after midnight. If we couldn't get back in to work by seven A.M. it would mean a fine or a jail sentence or both! We worked feverishly, but that motor just would not start.

Around three o'clock in the morning, and in broad daylight (being summer so far up north), we heard the noise of a motor out on the lake. It was a speedboat racing around and coming quite near to our shore. We waved and yelled until he noticed us and came in to our dock. He was a boat captain for one of the big shots. It was such a beautiful morning, he said, that he had just decided to take a ride. We explained our predicament and offered him money, or liquor, or food if he would take us back to the ski factory dock.

He thought about it for a while and then said he would tow us back. We were very much relieved that we would not only get to work on time, but also get the boat back to town. The driver would not accept anything from us; he just said he was glad to help.

I was able to avoid the consequences of ever being late to work, but we still felt far from secure. Arrests were happening more and more often, even among people we knew. Toivo Grandell had been one of the first; we didn't know him very well. But then there were others whom we did know, and we had no idea what they could have done to warrant arrest.

Among the first from the ski factory to be arrested was a big, good-looking Finn named Kalle Soderstrom who was a good friend of ours. Just a few weeks after he had been jailed, he appeared, to our surprise, at our door, free on a technicality. Kalle was an intelligent fellow with a good sense of humor, fun to be with. He told us a little of his life history. After fighting on the Red side during the Finnish Civil War,* he was given a long jail sentence in Finland. Being young, he was not executed but he suffered from the poor conditions and lack of food. Smoking was not allowed in the jail, he told us, so he developed a method of swallowing the smoke to remove the evidence. There was one guard whom he hated for reporting the smallest infractions, so Kalle would swallow the smoke and wait to burp it up in front of the guard. The man always smelled it, but could never find a cigarette on him so he got away with it. As he told us about it, he was smoking and swallowing the smoke. Then he demonstrated burping the smoke out. We could tell this had given him a lot of pleasure amid the horrible conditions he endured in prison.

Soderstrom's situation was especially uncertain because he had skipped the border from Finland when he came to Russia and, having a jail record there, he was sure he would face a prison term in Finland if he went back. Now he was also facing the possibility of being arrested again in Russia if he stayed. I'm sure if he had known the horrors that he

---

*The Finnish Civil War was fought from January to April of 1918. The Whites, or Constitutionalists, triumphed. Many of the Reds, which included Social Democrats as well as Bolsheviks, were imprisoned in Finland. Most of their leaders fled to Moscow or Karelia after the war.

would face if he was taken again in the Soviet Union, he would have tried to escape to Finland, but he didn't. Before long he was arrested again and that was the last we ever heard of him.

It was still in 1937 when Elias Tuomainen, the director of the ski factory, was arrested and I felt real bad about that. I knew him well and just couldn't understand what he could have done. In 1938 things got even worse for the Finns in Karelia. It seemed to me that most of the people being arrested were Finns not Karelians. Our old friend Heino was arrested, as was the band director, Elis Ranta. We just couldn't understand it. We knew these people were innocent of any wrong doing. When we asked people who were party members about the arrests, they assured us that anyone who was innocent would be freed. Keijo Frilund was one who said that. I asked him point blank if all these people could actually be guilty. I remember Keijo was sitting on our sofa, legs crossed and one foot waving up and down. "They must be," he said. Maybe he believed it—until he too was arrested. He never got out.

One weekend we went to Pässinranta with Ilmi and Keijo. Keijo had just returned from a trip up north where he had served as an interpreter at interrogations of people who had been arrested. He seemed different—almost like a changed person, more somber and quieter. Ilmi said she had noticed it too. He wasn't saying much and hung around her and little Irma a lot.

We were at home late one evening when suddenly Eino and Sylvi Dahlstrom burst into our room to tell us that Benny Laine was being arrested at that very moment. The Dahlstroms had been in town and, on their way home, had walked past the barracks where Benny and Miriam lived. They had a custom of whistling whenever they went by, and Benny or Miriam would open the window and say hello. On this evening, when Eino gave his shrill whistle, Miriam yelled out the window that the police were there and were taking Benny with them. Eino and Sylvi had raced directly to our place.

We were all devastated. It was so horrible. Although we knew many people who had been arrested, this just hit us really hard. It felt like this was the end, like maybe we would be next.

Benny was a Canadian. He had been brought to Karelia by his parents when he was just a kid. He didn't mess with politics or belong to any clubs. His interests were just his job as a mechanic at the ski factory and his family. He was one of the finest fellows I had the pleasure of working with; Sylvi and I often spent evenings with the Laines and Dahlstroms and shared a drink or two. So we were really in shock to learn of Benny's arrest. His father was arrested too, and to my knowledge neither one has been heard of since. Eino told me later that Ben had told him that the secret police had talked to him about becoming a spy for them. They would have trained him for the job but he turned them down. He wasn't supposed to tell anyone about it but he did tell Eino, who kept it secret until after Benny was arrested.

Things kept getting worse. In July of 1938 we had a night of horror known afterward among the Finns as "*suuri kauhu*" (the great terror). The NKVD was everywhere that night. We spent the whole night expecting their knock at our door, but it never came. We watched from the window as gunmen took some of our good friends away.

The next morning only a couple of Karelians and one Finn showed up for work in machine repair. The others, about twenty-three men, had been arrested. I still don't know why I wasn't taken, since I was the foreman in machine repair. Usually the leaders were taken first.

One Sunday soon after, we were at our summer place with Dave. He and Lily were openly divorced by this time. We noticed a motor boat pull up and stop at the ski factory dock in Pässinranta and thought it looked like the police. We quickly took to the woods taking some pans along and pretending to pick berries. After what seemed like a long time I decided to scout around and see what was happening. Dave didn't dare go because they had already been looking for him. He warned me, too. "You go out there and the first thing you'll do is get caught," he predicted. He was right.

I headed towards the cabin still pretending to pick berries. Suddenly a group of rifle-toting secret police came around a bend in the trail and spotted me. They wanted to know my name and proceeded to look through their papers. They had a very long list, but my name wasn't on it. They were very polite then, thanked me, and told me to go on picking berries while they went on to the next cabin. I hung around watching to see when they left so the rest could come out of hiding.

Pretty soon they returned down the trail with an old Finn by the name of Lintula limping along between them. As they passed me Lintula spoke out of the side of his mouth: "*Nyt se on vientiä, sanoi papukaija kissalle.*" ("It's the end of the line, said the parrot to the cat.") The old saying fit the circumstances well. "*Lintu*" is the Finnish word for "bird." Old man Lintula in the hands of the NKVD was just like a bird in the cat's mouth.

I went back to tell Sylvi and Dave that it was safe to come out; they had gone. Dave was sure that he was on their list. He had had a premonition one night that he was in line to be arrested and had gone out and slept in his chicken coop. Most of the arrests at this time occurred at night. It was easier to find people at home then, and there weren't so many others watching. Sure enough, the police had come looking for him that very night but, fortunately, didn't think to look in the coop. Soon after, Dave went to the cabin and planned his escape. He wanted us to come along, and I might have gone, but Sylvi was afraid. "You're going to kick yourself," Dave predicted.

Vilho and Terttu went with him. They left by rowboat from Pässinranta one night, intending to go along the shore to Solomanni and then up the river as far as possible before striking out through the woods with a compass to Finland. The morning after they left, an American-Finn named Erkkila came by the cabin in another boat. "They won't get far," he said. "I reported them."

We were appalled. Maybe he did it out of fear, hoping to get better treatment for himself. His wife had already been arrested; maybe he did it for spite. It was many years before we learned what had happened to Dave.

S: One evening during the summer of 1938, in the midst of the arrests, we were returning home from the Summer Park. It was late but, being summer, not dark. As we reached our courtyard we heard the radio, from an outside speaker, blaring out the notes of the "Internationale." At the same time we saw the police rounding up people from our barracks.

Until then, the "Internationale" to us had been an expression of hope for a better world in the future, for freedom from fear. But now, hearing its stirring notes and, at the same time, being witness to a mass arrest of friends and fellow workers horrified us. How could this be? We decided to go to Ilmi and Keijo's apartment; it would be a comfort to be with friends at such a time. But as we turned to go, we saw Ilmi at their window. "Don't come here," she called to us. "They are taking Keijo."

In our own room we spent a sleepless night waiting in terror for the knock at our door. The knock never came, but we felt sure it would some other night.

After that night we just knew that Lauri would be taken too. I was terrified. We made some preparations, planned what he would take with him if he had to go. I remember going by bus one day to see Lily who had told us she had a pair of very sturdy men's boots that we could have. I cried all the way. We could not understand why these people—mostly men and mostly people we felt we knew well—were being arrested. Viktor Viiki and Albin Heino were among them. We could not believe they were guilty of any wrongdoing.

L: After the big night of arrests at the ski factory there were many women left alone. Word came that these women should get ready to move so that their rooms could be used by couples. They would be taken, we were told, to a place where they would soon be reunited with their husbands. Even women with small babies had to go. Ilmi Frilund went with little Irma, and she was so happy, fully believing that Keijo would join them. They were all taken on to a big scow at the docks and then towed to an island on Lake Onega where lime was produced for industrial use. It turned out that the women were put to work there. No husbands ever showed up. It must have been the biggest disappointment of their lives. But they weren't exactly prisoners; many of them were back in town before fall. Ilmi Frilund returned and spent the winter at Pässinranta.

One of the ladies taken to the island was Katri Lammi, an actress and singer who worked at the Finnish Dramatic Theater in Petrozavodsk. Katri was married to a well-known singer, Jukka Ahti, who had been arrested some time earlier. They used to sing together a lot, which is what they had done while the police were searching their apartment before they arrested Jukka. Those who saw Katri leave for Lime Island said she put on quite a performance, having the police pack and carry her things onto the scow. Richly dressed in furs and laces from the theater, she paraded along the dock, singing parts from operas. Once on the island, Katri got the job of driving a horse hauling stone to the dock. People said she was a real sight, dressed in the most ridiculous way—furs, lace, muffs—and acting the part of some character. I wished I had seen it.

After her divorce, my cousin Lily married a man named John. He was also arrested and charged with espionage. He was made to stand in a corner facing it, and, as the guards walked by, they hit him in the back of the head so his face would hit the wall. He said it was much worse than seeing a blow coming and bracing for it. After enduring this treatment for some time he decided to admit guilt. Whatever they asked him he admitted doing, and, when they asked for names of accomplices, he gave them names. However, he made sure to give them only names of people he knew were already dead. He made his story so believable his interrogators were pleased. He remained in jail, but there were no more beatings.

The papers he had signed detailing his "crimes" were sent to the central headquarters. It was a few months before they discovered that his stories were all lies. At that point, they let him go, and he was not arrested again. They must have had their quota filled in Karelia by that time.

But most of the people who were taken were never seen or heard from again. None of our friends who were arrested ever returned. Either they perished in the concentration camps or else they received what the Finns called a "*viiden kopekaan tuomio*" (five-kopeck sentence) which meant that they were shot. Five kopecks was the price of a rifle bullet.

The Winter War

L: In the summer of 1938 we decided that we would try to get back to the United States. Many others would have liked to leave too, but most of our closest friends did not apply being sure they would be refused. Those who did apply did not tell everyone. They were afraid they might lose their jobs.

Our first question was whether we, who were now Soviet citizens, would be permitted to enter the United States. You couldn't even apply for release from the Soviet Union unless you already had permission to enter another country. Sylvi made a trip to the American Embassy in Moscow with her friend Flossie to find out if we could return to the United States. The answer was yes.

The next problem of course, was whether the Soviets would allow us to leave. There were all kinds of forms to fill out to get permission to emigrate, and many questions to answer, such as, "Why do you want to leave?" Many people felt that it was none of the government's business why they wanted to leave, and I agreed, but the government had all the power, and we had to play by their rules. For that question, we put down that my parents were poor and getting old. They needed our support, and we had no way to help them financially from the Soviet Union. We had just finished the application when Eino Dahlstrom walked in and read it. He said that helping our parents wouldn't mean a thing to these people. But we couldn't think of anything better for an answer, so we left it the way it was and sent it in. For a long time we heard nothing about it.

We did make another train trip to Moscow though, to tell the people at the American Embassy that we had applied to leave. This time I was able to go with Sylvi. While we were there we attended an agricultural show and an air show. I remember at the agricultural show we bought sandwiches and beer and the beer bottles were covered with bees from nearby hives that were part of the show. For entertainment they had a motorcycle barrel racing act. The drivers were American women.

We took a train to the air show, which was some distance from Moscow over a vast, open field. It lasted two or three hours. All kinds of aircraft—from fighter planes to helicopters—flew right over our heads. It struck me as very dangerous. There was a huge crowd of spectators. When the show was over, a train appeared to take people back to Moscow. Everyone rushed to catch the train. We had to go around a high wooden fence demarking the air field. In the mad rush, people started climbing the fence, and it came crashing down. The train was soon covered with people hanging on all over the place. Loudspeakers kept saying that the train couldn't start with so many on it and that another train would be coming soon, but no one listened. We waited in the shelter of a building. A young girl also took refuge there, coughing blood from having been crushed in the crowd. We couldn't understand how people could act that way. Better to walk to Moscow than get caught in that wild pack. Many people were injured that afternoon, but we never saw anything in the paper about it. Papers only printed what the government wanted them to print.

One thing we did read, in all the newspapers in Karelia during the time we were there, was that Nazi Germany was a horrible, repressive country and an enemy of the working class. So in August of 1939, when Stalin and Hitler signed their nonaggression pact, we did not know what to think. We had been told that Hitler was our enemy, so for most of us this unexpected pact was hard to take. But we had one electrician in the factory who caught on real fast to this about-face. He kept walking around bragging that with Germany as our ally, "nobody can beat us now!" He seemed real happy about it. I wish I could have seen him in June, 1941, when Hitler attacked the Soviet Union.

All through the summer of 1939 we saw freight train loads of war materiel being moved north. We could see tanks, trucks and cannons on flat cars and a lot of big boxes and barrels. We didn't know what was coming until later in the fall when newspapers began to talk about negotiations with Finland. Then in the latter part of November the Russian army attacked Finland and the "Winter War" was on.

Newspapers talked about the advances the Red Army was making on all fronts, especially the eighth army. They were going to go straight across Finland—cut it in two. They did advance during the first few weeks, but then they were stopped. Finnish ski troops were behind the Russian lines cutting down trees to block their supply lines. The Russians were trapped. I heard later that Finland's strategy was to let them come just so far and then try to get them to surrender, but the Russians just hung on even though they ran out of food and supplies. A lot of them died of hunger; it was a very cold winter.

Two men from our shop went with the eighth army, and one returned after the war ended in March of 1940. He told us what a terrible time they had had. The Soviet Air Force tried to fly in supplies, he said, but half the time the drops would miss them and fall to the enemy. The Finns had powerful radio speakers in the trees and would urge them, in Russian, to surrender, offering them so much for a rifle, a tank, a machine gun, any equipment. The situation became so desperate for the Soviets that they decided to escape on foot and fight their way out. Their ammunition was low, so they had to be careful with it, and the snow was hip deep. To survive, they had to eat their horses, but they couldn't build a fire or the Finns would see it and shoot. It was a very small group that finally got out.

The Russian army was transporting fuel to the front in barrels on regular trucks. Finnish ski troops would ambush the trucks. Without even bothering to attack the driver, they would simply shoot holes in the barrels so all he could do was turn around for another load.

They brought some of the shot-up barrels to the ski factory for repair and I was given the job of welding them while two men ran hot steam through them so they wouldn't explode from gas left in the seams. These men had been in the army and were wounded so they weren't sent back to the front. They were happy to help me and did a very good job; I didn't have a single one explode.

One of the soldiers helping me had been driving a tank. He told me that when word came to attack he thought to himself, "Helsinki, here I come." But soon after he hit a mine and landed in a field hospital.

The other fellow said he was a foot soldier. He had been wounded while trying to sneak up on a bunker. He was hit by shrapnel as he was crawling through the snow. He told me about a time when his platoon was trying to cross a river. Every little while, seemingly out of nowhere, someone would get shot. All day long they couldn't get ahead. At one time they thought they saw movement across the river and started firing with everything they had: tanks, cannon, small arms. Still, some people were getting hit.

Finally, late in the evening someone spotted a sniper in a tree. They shot it down and went to look. It was a woman.* She had been sitting in a hammock with a thermos bottle, lunch, chocolate bars and a scoped rifle with plenty of ammunition. He said it was just luck that they happened to notice her, she was so well camouflaged.

The ski factory was on full-time war work by now. They increased production, so quality suffered. The skis were at best a grade three by now as were the poles and the little sleds called *pulkkas* that were used to haul ammunition to the front lines and wounded to the rear. The name *pulkka* came from Finland. They were boat-shaped sleds that the Laplanders used, pulled by reindeer. They didn't sink deeply into the snow because of their shape and being made of wood; they were light weight and ideal for the foot soldier to pull behind him.

I was collecting three rubles for each barrel I repaired, plus my salary. Sometimes I would think about how the Finns were shooting holes in these barrels and here I was, an American Finn, patching them up. Why did things like that happen? We felt pride in the Finns but didn't talk about it much, even with close friends. Someone might inadvertently say something that could get us in trouble. Over near the ski factory club house was a fenced area where Finnish prisoners were kept. I saw one man in there, and I really wanted to go and talk to him, but knew I'd better not. Somebody might see. We were still living with fear.

The Winter War lasted 105 days, ending with the Treaty of Moscow signed on March 13, 1940. Of course Finland, with 4,000,000 people was no match for the Soviet colossus with 180,000,000 inhabitants. The wonder was that the Finns were able to hang on so long and inflict so much damage as they did on the Red Army. In the end, Finland lost about ten percent of her territory. Most of the people who had lived in the ceded areas relocated within the new Finnish borders rather than live under Soviet rule.

---

*Many Finnish women helped in the war effort, though usually not at the front. They were known as the "Lottas."

What Are They Giving?

S: By 1939 things had quieted down and we went on with our lives. Stalin's non-aggression pact with Hitler stunned us; we could not understand how a communist nation could be friendly with a fascist country. As Lauri has written, we saw the preparations which were being made at the Finnish border as the trains rolled by Petrozavodsk with supplies for the Red Army. The Winter War brought various changes into our daily lives. Although the Red Army expected to walk right through to Helsinki, precautions were taken, nevertheless, in case of enemy air raids. We had to cover our windows with heavy blankets when evening came and lights were turned on. We also took turns being guards outside each barracks and wore armbands to distinguish ourselves. Our guard duty consisted of checking all windows to make sure no light was showing through. Then, too, all radios had to be turned in to the authorities. This was probably done to prevent us from hearing any propaganda from the Finns or making any contact with them.

My friend Tyyne and I had an amusing experience one day soon after the Red Army had attacked Finland. Since we carried water by the bucketful into our rooms and also carried slop water out the same way, bathing at home was not easy. But we had public baths in town with different sections for men and women. Tyyne and I were standing in line for the bath one day when we overheard a couple of Red Army men in the other line. One of them said, "Well in a couple of weeks we will be having a bath in Helsinki." We know now that it was years before they could have had their bath, and, even then, it would have had to be as tourists, not as conquerors.

Our radios were returned to us after the Winter War, but the airwaves were often jammed by the Soviets. We did sometimes get music from Finland, and it sounded good to us. We especially enjoyed it one evening when we heard "Ain't She Sweet?" a song that had been popular when we were still in the States, sung with a strong Finnish accent.

The Finnish language was brought back into use in 1940, but as far as I was concerned, my teaching days were over. After I left the teaching job in the Russian school in 1937, I became a homebody and spent my time keeping house (in one little room?) and standing in queues (*ochereds*, in Russian) to get food.

At this time I became good friends with Tyyne Nurminen who was also a stay-at-home. Her husband, Viljo, was a party member, and I never had felt at ease with him, but Tyyne was very outgoing and friendly and a lot of fun. They had a little boy born in March of 1938 who became very dear to us. He was our little Heikki (Henry). He treated us as another set of parents and loved to be with us. To differentiate between me and our friend Sylvi Dahlstrom whom he also knew, he'd call me "*meijän syyvi*" (our Sylvi) and her, "*Dalsto syyvi*" or Dahlstrom's Sylvi.*

While Tyyne was trying to toilet train him, she came over one day and announced in triumph that she had taught Heikki a marvelous new trick. When I asked to see it, she removed his diaper, helped him stand up and lo and behold, he peed on our floor! I was not nearly as elated with his trick as she was—but I loved him dearly.

One day when Heikki was about two and a half years old, he strayed from the barracks area. Tyyne and I searched all over town and no Heikki. On the way downtown we had to cross a little river and we were fearful of what might have happened to him. Finally we went to the police and tearfully told them our story. One of them grinned at us and said, "Don't worry, those little ones always turn up. It's when your big boys are missing that you have to worry." We were disgusted with their

*Finns often call a person by their last name in the possessive form, followed by their first name, as in, Hokkasen Lauri or Dahlstromin Sylvi.

uncaring attitude, but Heikki did turn up, none the worse for his escapade.

Heikki was often with us at mealtime, and once, after we'd all had some potato soup, he held up his dish and said, "Give me some more of that potato water." He was right: it was potatoes, onions and water. You couldn't fool him.

During our first summer in northern Karelia, our food had consisted of dried potatoes, canned meat and porridge, bread, of course, with sometimes a bit of milk. After moving to Petrozavodsk we were able to buy more and better food, especially while the INSNAB store for foreigners was open. I remember a date-filled cooky that was delicious, and a pastry called Napolean . . . scrumptious . . . and plain shortbread-type cookies. Fresh meat was very scarce, and we would often make meatloaf from sausage which was more available. We could buy prunes, but found them inedible because instead of being dried, they had been smoked. Potatoes were diced and dried. Once on a hunting trip Lauri and Eino had the good luck to buy a quantity of potatoes, but they froze on the way home. Fruits were non-existent, as were fresh vegetables. The staples were available but we had to stand in long lines for them.

When food was in small supply, there was the tendency for people to get what they could and hoard it. Whenever we came across a food line, we would check it out. The regular procedure was this: first we found the end of the line and asked in Russian, "*Kto posledniy?*" ("Who is last?") Then we said, "*Ya za vami,*" ("I'm after you,") and, finally, asked, "*Shto dayut?*" ("What are they giving?"). Of course they weren't "giving" anything, but one was lucky to be able to buy anything at all.

Tyyne and I usually went together through these food lines. Often we would stand in line all night waiting for the store to open and "give" us a kilo of meat or sugar. In the bitter cold of winter, we would take turns going home to warm up and then returning again to our place in line. One day Tyyne told me that her husband had asked her why I was hoarding so much food. Since Tyyne was with me practically all the time buying as much, if not more, food than I did, I was incensed by the question, and she and I quarreled. We did not speak to each other or stand in any lines together for some time. Finally one day, as I turned a corner at the shopping mall downtown, I ran straight into Tyyne. Our quarrel was forgotten; we embraced and spent many an hour together again.

The scarcity of food often made people act like animals in their fear of being left without, and there was danger of being trampled under foot by those determined to get into a store the minute the doors were opened whether they had stood in line or not. I remember a time when I was in line with Sylvi Dahlstrom where people were pushing and shoving. When the doors opened a crowd swept us in, and I fainted dead away from the pressure. Several people came to my aid, however, and I got whatever was being sold without having to wait any longer.

Another time Tyyne and I were in a very unruly crowd with the most aggressive ones pushing their way in every time the door opened leaving those of us in line waiting outside. It looked hopeless. But for some reason, Lauri had come downtown to look for us, and he took it upon himself to get next to the door and stand guard, keeping the line in order until Tyyne and I got in. Then he let go, came in after us, and let the devil take the hindmost.

A crowd of people that otherwise and elsewhere was well-behaved could, if conditions were right, turn into an ugly mob with only one selfish aim: to attain whatever it was they wanted at the moment. Even law-abiding citizens could forget their scruples and join the crowd. Having been caught up in several of these hysterical groups during our stay in Karelia, I am still wary and frightened of large crowds and will not willingly join them.

Although at first the foreigners did have much better food than the natives, after INSNAB closed we were no better off. The sour black bread, "*buhanka*," in Russian, was hard on one's digestive system. Many Americans and Finns, especially Americans, developed stomach ailments. I did, and had to see doctors for help. One of them had me taking hydrochloric acid, which had to be taken so it did not touch my teeth. Normally this acid is present in one's stomach in a very dilute form but mine must have been lacking it. I have never since been told by any doctor about such a problem. The doctors in the Soviet Union were mostly women, and I remember being mighty disgusted with one of them who was much more interested in the ring I was wearing than in my complaints.

But those of us who had come to the Soviet Union to build a workers' paradise had been willing to carry on that work as best we could, in spite of the meager and nearly indigestible food and primitive living conditions. It was only when our freedom was threatened and then taken away that some of us—not all—lost our illusions and realized that our dream was not going to work.

The Family Needs Us

L: For a long time we heard nothing about our application to leave the Soviet Union. We had sent it in late in 1938. We even wrote a letter to the Supreme Soviet trying to expedite the matter. Finally in December of 1940 we received a notice to report to a certain address on a certain date in connection with our application to leave the country. When we nervously presented ourselves we were asked again why we wanted to leave. I said, again, that my parents had no way to support themselves and needed us. We were then told that our application had been approved and we had permission to leave. We would be given the necessary papers and information on how to proceed.

At first, it was hard to believe that we would actually be able to leave. When we told some of our friends about it, they cautioned us to go easy and not get our hopes up too high. As far as we know, there was only one other American-Finnish family besides us from Petrozavodsk that received permission to leave. The rest got letters saying, "You do not have enough reason to leave." We had to sign a paper that we would never return to the Soviet Union.

In spite of the skepticism of our friends, we could not help getting enthused about our return. It was in our minds every day, as was the fear that something would happen to dash our hopes. Not long after we got our permit, I got a notice to report to NKVD headquarters at a certain time in the evening. I was not told what it was all about, just to come as directed, and I was really worried. Were we going to be able to go home or not?

Arriving at the appointed time, I was directed to a room and told to wait. Soon an officer came in, introduced himself, and asked me to sit down. Then he asked me about a book by Sinclair Lewis called *It Can't Happen Here* which had been published in the States in 1935. How did I get the book, he wanted to know, what did I think of it, and did I have it now.

We had gotten that book from Ilmi Frilund. When she had to leave her rooms and go to Lime Island she asked us if we would take care of some of their books until she had a place for them. We did, of course, and the Lewis book was among them. Some time later, our band director's son-in-law came over and wanted to borrow it, and we let him have it. I told all this to my interrogator and also that I hadn't read it very well but knew that it was a fictional story about fascism coming to America. Everything I said was written down and then he read it out loud to me, and I signed it.

Then came the surprise. They brought in the young man who had borrowed the book, his hands cuffed behind his back. He was very pale, looked tired, and I noticed he did not sit until he was told to.

The interrogator introduced us and asked the prisoner to tell his version of the story about the book. He took a deep breath, then exhaled, as if he had told his story over and over. When he was through, the officer asked me if I agreed with everything he had said. I said yes, only that I had not told the young man about the book; he had asked if we had it. I made that clear because I remembered that this was what I had told him earlier. I couldn't really see what difference it made, but I knew one had to be careful, and I sensed that there had to be something they didn't like in that book.

After the prisoner was taken away the officer thanked me for coming in to talk to him and said that was all he wanted. As I was leaving I asked him what this was all about, and he said that the book was anti-Soviet and makes fun of Stalin. When I thought about it I could understand how they might see it that way because what was happening in Russia at the time was very similar to that depicted in the book: paranoia had set in and people were afraid for their lives. Actually, "it can't happen here" is exactly what we would have thought, back in 1935 or 1936, about many of the things that *did* happen in Karelia in 1937 and 1938.

In January 1941, I received orders to go to a powerhouse that was furnishing power for the Iljinski sawmill on the shore of Lake Ladoga. I was asked to do some welding on a smokestack that was in danger of collapse. Why they asked me, I don't know. I did know that if you refused, it could or would be held against you. I was told that I could negotiate my pay when I got there.

I left Petrozavodsk by train getting off at a small station about half way to Leningrad. There was an open pick-up truck waiting for me. It was about a three-hour ride and very cold, but I was prepared for it, knowing my job would be outside.

The following morning I was shown the job. There were five-eighths-inch by three-foot by six-foot supports to be welded all around the stack, but there was no welding rod made up. The first job was to cut some three thirty-seconds mild steel into lengths, make a coating to dip them into and then dry them. I had a helper to stand up the supports while I tac-welded them. Then, while I was welding, he made welding rods.

I got my power directly from the power house. There was a rheostat on the panel in the power house. Someone had to sit there and keep the current at a certain gauge reading because, when I would strike an arc, it would draw the current down. If the person wasn't on the ball, I would have a rough time. There were several women there; I asked if anyone could speak Finnish, and finally a Karelian woman spoke up, so I gave her the job.

After a few tries I found a satisfactory heat setting and explained to her that while I was welding she must keep the amp needle right on the mark. She caught on real fast, and we were a good team.

On the afternoon of the second day I started to have trouble maintaining the arc. It got worse as I went along, so I went inside to see what was wrong and found a young fellow sitting in her place at the rheostat. When I asked the foreman what was going on, he just said the old lady was back on her regular job in the lumber yard. I insisted that she be brought back, or I wouldn't be doing any more welding. It wasn't long before she showed up, all smiles. I felt better too. We put in long hours, and the work progressed satisfactorily.

The decking on which I was welding got wet when it snowed due to the heat from the smoke so they gave me a pair of rubbers to wear over my felt boots. When it came time for my pay they were going to charge me for them, but I protested, and they let me keep them. I did not have to pay for my board and room either, which was a plus, and I was given permission to shop at their special store for technical workers so my pack had candy, cookies, cigarettes and tea—things that were hard to get. They came in handy on the way back home to Petrozavodsk.

The money part I knew would be a stickler. When time came for my pay, I had it all planned in advance. So the negotiations wouldn't take too long, I merely asked for twenty percent more than I thought was a fair price. After a little bargaining, I let them cut it, and everyone was happy. The director shook hands with me, said he was pleased with the job and wished me well.

I rode back to the train station the same way, in the pick-up truck. We stopped at an old farmhouse to warm up. The lady of the house put the samovar on the table and soon we had tea. She was Karelian so I was able to converse with her in Finnish. She told me that she was alone with her four kids; her husband had been killed in the war, and the money she got from the government was so little that she had to make a little more by fixing tea water for travelers. At that time everyone carried their lunch and tea with them.

While we were having tea and lunch I saw some movement behind the brick oven they used for heating and baking. I asked her where the kids were. Sure enough, they were behind the stove where it was warm. She told them to come out, but they were so shy and afraid they would just peek out and dash back in. Finally one of them came out when I kept coaxing her with the cookies. She was pitfully thin, just skin and bones. After a lot of coaxing from me and their mother, they took a cookie and ran back to their hiding place. When it was time to go I left most of my goodies with the poor lady to feed those kids. They just got to me. I will never forget them.

I got back to Petrozavodsk on the 13th of January, Sylvi's birthday. I had been gone five days.

S: As the time came for our departure from the land that had been home for six and a half years, I became more and more nervous. Would we really be allowed to leave or would some red tape or technicality be used to keep us back? When Lauri was sent to the Iljinski sawmill, I was beside myself with worry, afraid that he would not return, that it was a trick of some kind. My friend Edla Joki stayed with me that first night to calm me down. When Lauri returned five days later, bearded and dirty, I was overjoyed to see him and felt that it was the best birthday present I'd ever received.

We sold or gave away all our belongings and most of our clothes to friends. Many of them had asked for certain things when they learned we were trying to leave, and they insisted on paying for them. I remember a lady who asked for our water kettle months before our departure. Our alarm clock, which we had brought from the States and which Lauri had repaired several times, was a thing of great value. Clocks were not available in the stores.

Our friends all stayed close to us although there was a stigma attached to folks who left, and they could have been judged guilty by association. We had a group of good, true friends there, and it was sad to leave them. I remember a group of us sitting on the floor in our room—perhaps the last night of our stay—having a farewell drink from glasses that already belonged to someone else. A glass was accidently broken and someone exclaimed, "*Sirpaleet tarkoittaa onnea.*" ("Broken glass foretells happiness.") But one of the company was more wary; he said, "You can't be sure you're out until the last railroad tie is behind you." I didn't need his warning; I was frightened enough as it was.

As far as we could tell, this group who sat with us the last night of our stay in Petrozavodsk was ideologically very much like us. They had come to the Soviet Union with their parents, most of them in their teens. They could not have been deeply imbued with communist ideas, and probably didn't understand the term any better than we did. Sure, we all knew that the communist state would be all that a worker would want and that we were striving for that in the Soviet Union. However, by this time we had seen and experienced many things that did not jibe with what we considered a workers' country. There had been arrests among friends, persecutions, the Stalin personality cult . . . how could these phenomena fit in with communism? We had questions which we dared not voice even to friends. But the questions were in our minds. These friends who sat with us that night were there to wish us well; some of them wished they could go with us, but, since they could not, they were glad for us. It hurt deeply to leave them. We had no way of knowing what terrible experiences lay ahead for them.

L: We were told we could buy tickets to the closest port in a foreign country with rubles. From then on we had to have foreign currency, which we could not obtain in Russia. Also, we were not allowed to take any rubles out of Russia, and they wouldn't have been of any value elsewhere anyway. All we were allowed to do was to change enough rubles for twenty American dollars to take with us. Think of it. After working for over six years in the country, twenty dollars, plus our few possessions, were all we had to take with us.

Since the war was on in Europe, we had to go east to Japan. So we wrote to my parents in Michigan asking them to have $50.00 and two boat tickets from Japan to California sent to the American Embassy in Kobe, Japan. Then we bought train tickets to Moscow. When we left Petrozavodsk on February 8 all we had left to our name was contained in one big suitcase except my shotgun and the clothes on our backs.

We spent that last night in Petrozavodsk with my cousin Lily and her husband, John. I had signed over our share in the cabin at Pässinranta to them. In the morning, Lily walked to the train station with us. When we got there I remembered that I had forgotten my shotgun so I went back to Lily's for it. Her daughter Viola had stayed home with her baby. She was crying, because we were leaving and probably because she would have liked to leave too. I gave her a hug, feeling really bad for her, and left again for the station with my gun. As things turned out, I should have just left the gun with Lily and John.

On the way to Moscow, we spent one day in Leningrad with our good friends Inkeri and Paul Kokko. (It was Inkeri's father who had hanged himself after being stripped of his party membership.) Paul had a young brother named Jyry who lived with them, and they also had a two-year-old daughter, a real charmer, who would crawl under the table to calm herself whenever she was disturbed. The family was doing well. Paul, who was from Detroit, was an army officer, and so they had better food and lodging than the average citizens.

Paul had done some translating during the Winter War. A Finnish army officer had been wounded and taken prisoner and was held in the hospital. He was a quadriplegic. Paul went to talk to him. As a fellow officer, he asked if there was anything he could do to help. The man looked at him hard before replying, "*Painu helvettiin sinä Ryssän kätyri.*" ("Go to hell you Russian traitor.") He meant, of course, that Paul, having become a Russian officer, was a traitor to his Finnish background. Paul could understand the Finnish officer's feelings. Before we left Leningrad

Paul gave me a pair of Russian army boots that I wore all the way to Japan (where it was finally too warm). I gave him my wrist watch, and Sylvi gave Inkeri hers.

Paul also warned me that the NKVD had agents operating in the United States. He advised me to keep a low profile at first because they were dangerous and could cause us a lot of grief.*

In Moscow we stayed with Evert Muukkonen and his wife, Katri, until we could find a hotel. (Katri had gone to school with Sylvi in Petrozavodsk.) They lived in an apartment building for auto workers, as did Martha and Dave Nieminen whom we knew from Detroit. (Martha was our good friend Paul Middleton's sister.) Dave didn't like the idea that we were leaving the Soviet Union and said so. He felt that we were deserting the workers' cause. I saw him at a bus stop in Moscow, and he asked me, "Why in the world are you leaving? There's no reason to leave." I didn't even try to tell him; he was very upset and didn't want to talk about it.

We were more comfortable with the Muukkonens who felt as we did about the arrests. They knew many who had been arrested and confided to us that they believed that most of them had been innocent of any crime against the state.

The first morning in Moscow we went to the United States embassy to see if our tickets and money had arrived in Japan. The embassy staff was very nice to us. Nothing had been received but they told us to keep checking.

Then we went to find a hotel, and luck was with us. There was a long line to register, and they were calling names in order. Shortly after we arrived they called a Polish man who wanted something cheaper than the room they offered him. So then they asked if anyone else would want that room; it was 100 rubles a day. I snapped it up, and we were escorted to a very nice suite: two rooms and a bath. It must have looked odd for us to take such an expensive room. The other travelers, judging by their clothes and luggage, were quite well-to-do. We didn't have much, but what we did have was in rubles and we couldn't take it with us so we figured we might as well live it up.

As soon as we were settled, we sent a telegram to my home asking why our tickets were delayed. A few days later, when they still hadn't come, we sent another. We were really getting worried since we wouldn't be allowed to leave unless there were money and tickets for us in Japan.

*Kaarlo Tuomi, a former KGB agent, agrees that Paul was right in warning us.

A couple of days after the third telegram was sent, on Washington's birthday, February 22, we arrived at the American Embassy to find a lot of smiling faces. The people there had been just as concerned as we were about our tickets and were very happy to tell us that they were finally safely at the American Embassy in Japan. What a great day that was. Everyone was so nice to us.

Later we learned what had taken so long. As soon as she heard from us, my mother had gone to the telegraph office in Sault Ste. Marie, Michigan, and given them the money to send to Japan for us.* Days later she received our telegrams and took a friend with her back to town to find out why we had not received the money. They discovered that the telegraph office had never sent it! Firmly anti-communist, they just didn't want to send money to help anyone in the Soviet Union. Mother and her friend got really angry and raised a big fuss. That got some action.

We had no trouble at all at the Japanese Embassy in Moscow. They gave us visas without question after we explained why we had to travel through Japan.

Then we had to buy our tickets from Moscow to Japan and there we ran into trouble. The bureaucrat in charge at the travel agency told us that we would have to have foreign currency to buy tickets to Japan. I protested. We had been recruited to come to the Soviet Union, I said, had worked there nearly seven years and had no dollars.

"Can you prove that you were recruited," he asked.

I had no idea how to do this but he suggested that we go to the archives where we should be able to find a record of it. We were a bit dubious but there seemed to be no other way so we took off. After much walking and asking of directions we located the huge building known as the archives. An extensive search of the inside brought us to some people who worked there. When we explained what we wanted and for what purpose they were amazed. It would take weeks, they guessed, possibly months, to find the papers we wanted, if they could be found at all. We gave up and returned to the travel bureau but the answer was still no.

Believing that there had to be something we could do to get through this impasse, we told our predicament to everyone who would listen. Someone suggested we try a certain law office where we were directed

---

*The tickets and the money amounted to $600. Some of this money came from the estate left by Sylvi's father. Indians using his farm house after Arvo left paid Evi fourteen dollars per month which she banked. The rest of the money she borrowed from a friend.

to a window. We knocked and a lady slid the window open and asked if she could help.

We explained that we were leaving to go back to the United States but had no dollars and that the travel agent refused to sell us tickets for Russian money. We told her how he had sent us to the archives to obtain proof that we had been recruited to come to the Soviet Union. She appeared hardly able to believe our story. The travel agent, she said positively, had to sell us tickets, and she would personally see to it that he did. She told us to go right back and get the tickets, and she would call the agent.

So back we went to the travel bureau where we found the agent still adamant in his refusal to sell. Then back to the lady at the law office who was equally adamant that he would sell! The shuffle continued. It was on about our fourth visit to the law office, when the lady became really upset, grabbed the phone, and shouted some things I couldn't make out. Then she said to me, "You go back there right now and, if he won't sell, come right back and tell me."

I walked into the ticket office, and the agent threw the tickets across the desk at me. I threw the money back at him and walked out. I guess he just wanted to cause trouble for people who were leaving. Maybe he was even jealous. Or, just possibly, he was looking for a chance to pocket some foreign currency.

While we were staying at the hotel in Moscow a young couple came to visit us. We knew the girl from Detroit; she had moved to the Soviet Union with her parents and married a Russian fellow. He seemed very nice, and we were pleased that she had found such a good and fun-loving husband. When I mentioned to him that I was taking my shotgun back home with me, he thought I would probably not be able to get it through customs. He asked if he could buy it. I agreed to sell it and named a price. He didn't have any money on him but promised to pay the next day. The following day he called and explained that he couldn't get the money to us just then but would send it by telegram to Vladivostok, and we could pick it up when we got there. I began to smell a rat, but there wasn't much we could do. I should have known better, especially since he had stuffed a whole place setting of silverware from the hotel into his shirt when they left. When we protested he just laughed and said they'd never miss it.

This gave us one more thing to worry about. We did check the telegraph office in Vladivostok and even sent him a telegram. All we got out of the whole business was a good lesson.

We also were entitled to exchange forty rubles for twenty dollars American for landing money in a foreign port. The bank in Moscow made out a permit for us to present to customs in Vladivostok which would allow us to take the twenty dollars out of Russia. We did have another $20 American, plus some change, acquired from selling our possessions to American friends in Petrozavodsk. This we hoped to take with us one way or another.

The trans-Siberian railroad was to take us to Vladivostok, a nine-day trip with brief stops for fuel, crew changes and to pick up and unload passengers and supplies. We took a sleeping coach; our compartment had four bunks that we had to share with others. I slept in one top bunk with Sylvi in the lower. Across from us were two men: a Russian army officer and a diplomat courier traveling through Japan and the United States to England.

The coach was warm, even in forty below Celsius. After a few days we got to know our roommates better and were more relaxed. But we needed exercise. All we could do was walk the length of the coach back and forth on one side; the other side was divided into sleeping compartments.

The food in the dining car was simple: no greens, just soups, porridge, bread, and tea. We became constipated, at times so badly that we couldn't eat. Sylvi especially suffered from it. So we were counting the days.

The landscape was interesting. Thousands of miles of snow, tundra, trees, mountains, and prairie passed by. There were a few towns and an occasional village with people heavily bundled against the bitter cold. Only their weatherbeaten faces showed, what we would call the layered look.

All the towns had tiny stores called *kiosks*. They were so small that the customers didn't even go inside. They would just go to a window, or "*fortochka*," where they paid and received their merchandise: bread, sugar or rice. The *kiosk*, which was unheated, would remain open until they sold out and then close until the next shipment. At one railroad stop I watched a woman purchase two loaves of bread from one of these *kiosks*. Having no bag, she slipped off one of her petticoats and wrapped the bread in it. Better than letting it freeze.

About two thirds of the way across Siberia, we were nearing Lake Baikal. I noticed we were getting into high country and going through a lot of tunnels. At one point we were actually headed back towards Moscow in order to get around the lake. Lake Baikal claimed the distinction of being the deepest lake in the world. We were able to buy some smoked fish at a stop near the lake—it was delicious. It looked like herring or whitefish. From Lake Baikal the railroad continued easterly to Khabarovsk where it turned south for about four hundred miles to Vladivostok, where we arrived on March 6, 1941, nine days after leaving Moscow.

We got ourselves a hotel room, but it was a real mess. There was only one toilet on our floor, and it was blocked up, stinking so bad we hated to go near it. After getting situated, we checked over our papers and had an unpleasant surprise. The paper from the bank allowing us to exchange rubles for American money to take across the border was dated to expire a few days before we were to sail.

We went first to the American Consulate both to let them know we were there and to tell them about our post-dated permit. The vice consul said there was nothing he could do about it. When I started to say more he put his finger near his lips and inclined his head toward his secretary to caution me to go easy. The secretary was a Russian, and the vice consul apparently felt that he could report our conversation to NKVD authorities who might keep us from leaving. Then he wished us good journey for the rest of the way. I read recently that Angus I. Ward was the United States consul general in Vladivostok in 1941. I wish I had known then that he was from Chassel, Michigan.

We sent telegrams to the bank in Moscow about our permit, as well as some to the gun buyer but had no results in either case.

The day before we were to leave, I asked a Polish engineer who was traveling through Russia to the United States if he would take twenty American dollars through customs for us since he had a permit. He agreed.

At customs the next day I pretended that I didn't know that the permit had expired and just handed it in. The agent took such a quick glance before telling me it was no good that I felt certain he knew in advance it would be expired, as if there was some kind of conspiracy between the bank in Moscow and the customs office in Vladivostok. I had to fork over the twenty dollars that was necessary for landing in Japan. I still had maybe two dollars in American change and the Polish engineer to fall back on.

I will never forget how it felt when we left the harbor at Vladivostok on March 11. We were moving through ice but gradually beginning to feel free as the ship pulled away from the shore. It was hard to believe that we were actually going home at last!

Immigrants Again

L: There were three classes on the Japanese ship we took to Kobe: First class was above decks, second below and the third was down in the hold. They were all displaced persons in the hold, mostly Jews from Poland running from the Nazis. I don't know how they got to Vladivostok. The men would get out on deck, form a circle and dance and sing holding on to each other. I didn't see any of the women or children join them. We heard that Japan did not accept them; they were sent back to Vladivostok on the same ship but later a Jewish organization got them to Hong Kong.

In second class we were jammed four to a small room with barely room to turn around. The Polish engineer and one other man shared our room. We slept three nights in that room, the last anchored just outside the Japanese port to wait for customs in the morning. We had had meal tickets issued on the ship. The young man who was serving was very concerned about collecting these. He kept saying "tickee no, eating no." The food was poor.

The mess hall where we took our meals had long tables seating ten or twelve, and it also served as a sitting room. As we were lounging there one evening; our Polish engineer came in. As he walked by the young waiter who was fussing with the tables, he gave him a light kick with the side of his foot. I could see the young man got very upset. He soon took off and came back with another member of the crew who appeared ready to fight. He advanced toward the engineer swinging his arms and yelling in Japanese. I was sure he would beat up on the Pole who was backing away and trying to explain that he meant no harm. Then the captain walked in and just stood there watching, apparently enjoying the proceedings. Finally the Japanese wild man gave up, and they left. Our engineer was very subdued after that. He was so scared that when we went to bed, he propped a chair against the door. To me that made about as much sense as the kicking in the first place.

On the morning of March 13th we landed in Tsuruoka, Japan. It was the most beautiful sight we had seen in years—like a fairyland. Everything was so green; fruit trees were in blossom and flowers were everywhere. The weather was warm.

Only one matter was bothering us. How would we be able to land without the $50 landing money? The Polish engineer, once on board the ship, had given me $10. He said he was short and would send me the rest of the money from Chicago, but that was the last of that ten dollars. I even reminded him by letter but he never responded. By that time, however, we were so happy to be back home that we didn't sweat the small stuff.

That morning in Tsuruoka we had ten Japanese yen given to me by the Russian diplomat we got to know on the train. We also had about twelve dollars American. The customs officials came on board ship to examine us. There were two lines: one for English speaking, the other for Russian. The English line was longer so we took the Russian.

When I was called in I found four examiners sitting around a table. They very politely asked me to sit down. The man on my left did most of the talking. He wanted to know what I thought of the Russians and what kind of mechanics they were. I said they were very poor mechanics. This brought a big laugh which made me feel better. I opened a box of expensive Russian cigarettes and offered it to the head man. As he was handing it back I motioned to him to pass it on, and when it returned to me I just pushed it over to my left.

Now we were all smoking in a relaxed atmosphere, and I knew just what to say. When they inquired about landing money I said we had 100 Japanese yen, some American money and more money at the American embassy in Kobe. They did not ask me to show any of it and wished me a pleasant trip. (We did have $50 from my parents at the embassy. If they had asked to see the 100 yen I would have pulled out the ten and claimed I thought it was a hundred. Fortunately, I didn't have to.)

We must have looked a sight as we boarded the train for Kobe, Sylvi in a fur coat and boots and I in heavy wool overcoat, fur hat and knee length boots plus a heavy shirt. The train left right on time, seemed to travel fast and arrived in Kobe at the expected minute. To us, it was amazingly efficient and clean, and we enjoyed it all. The countryside was interesting, and I relaxed from all the hassle, feeling that from then on things would get better for us.

On the 14th of March we arrived in Kobe and got a really nice room with a bath in which we luxuriated. The next morning, the cleanest we'd been for many days, we presented ourselves at the American Embassy and received the $50 that had been sent to us. They advised us to get the earliest ship we could find to the United States because so many people were leaving.

At the American President lines we learned that we were already booked on a ship leaving in three weeks. We could leave in two, however, if we were willing to take a third class berth on another vessel. We would have second class privileges. Considering how little money we had, we decided to change our tickets to the earlier boat, the S.S. *President Taft*.

We couldn't afford to stay on at the hotel but we found a nice, clean place at the YMCA for a dollar a day. There was no cooking, so we ate out: lots of rice at every meal, fish and some meat. We were so starved for fruit that we ate a big bag of it every day. The bananas seemed to be the best I'd ever tasted.

I ran into one of the other passengers on the ship from Vladivostok, a Jewish fellow who had traveled first class. He asked when we would be leaving Japan, and when I told him, offered to take us out for a sukiyake dinner.

It was a very good dinner. He and his wife were very nice to us, and we enjoyed their company, the sake, and the sukiyake very much. The meat was cooked in an electric skillet right at our table. Rice was served separately, and also some whipped raw egg. A little Japanese girl served us and showed us how to use the chop sticks. She placed them in our fingers and, giggling, motioned us to eat. I was a poor learner and got more of her attention than the rest—too much, in Sylvi's eyes. The idea was to take a piece of meat between the sticks, dip it in the raw egg and eat it. If I failed to get a piece into my mouth the waitress was right there to help.

After dinner our host got down to business. He asked if I would change some yen into dollars for him when we were leaving. There was a limit as to the amount a person was allowed to take out of the country; I think it was $100. Just before sailing, when everything was in order, a person took his yen to the bank and received dollars at the going exchange rate. This man was already dealing in the black market after only a few days in Kobe. We didn't have much money to change for ourselves so I changed fifty dollars for him. He was right at the bank door when I came out, not on the street as we had agreed.

We never felt any fear as we walked the streets of Kobe, even at night. We often stopped at little stores to shop for trinkets. The clerks would be sitting in the back; you'd have to go after them if you wanted to buy something. In the two weeks we were there we saw no crime and never a lock on a door. The money was difficult to understand; at first we simply handed over a pile of money and let clerks pick out the coins.

At that time the truck and car traffic wasn't heavy, and a lot of deliveries were done by bicycle. We saw people with six to eight pop or beer cases stacked on top of the bike rack. It was amazing how they balanced the load, and I never did get to see how they unloaded.

One day, looking around, we saw a bird store with the name *Takala* in big letters. "Must be a Finn," we thought, and went inside. There were all kinds of birds in there but only one man, and he was definitely not a Finn.

Our money was getting low so we pawned Sylvi's caracul fur coat for thirty-five dollars. Then we got her a summer coat and some silk material that was supposed to be cheaper than in the states.

Finally it was time to leave. We lined up on the dock for luggage inspection. There was no problem with ours but an American engineer near us was bringing home a samovar he had bought in Russia. The inspector opened the box and discovered a set of instructions and the price tag. These he threw in the harbor, but the samovar itself was all right to take.

Our third class sleeping quarters were bad, especially when the weather got rough. The second class food was excellent, however, and I sure enjoyed it, but poor Sylvi was seasick for many days. When seasick a person doesn't want to eat, and, if he did, he'd throw it up and get sicker.

It was evening when we arrived in Honolulu a few days later. Every place was closing up so we just walked around town a bit and sat in a park. The weather was warm and felt so nice; when we got back to the ship we took some blankets and slept up on the top deck.

The next morning we pulled out for San Francisco and in a few days hit some really rough weather. One morning I was the only one at breakfast. With four waiters at my command I really pigged out on grapefruit, eggs, bacon, sausage, cakes and coffee.

It had been March 29, 1941, when we left Japan. On the 12th of April, which was Good Friday that year, we finally sighted the Golden Gate bridge. From a distance it looked like a string pulled across the entrance to San Francisco Bay. The closer we got, the more beautiful it looked. To me it seemed like one of the great wonders of the world and held the promise of a new life for us in the future.

As we got closer the traffic became visible, and then it seemed as if our masts would not clear, but the *President Taft* slid easily under the bridge. What an unforgettable sight—the first glimpse of the good old United States of America. It is hard for me to describe the feelings I had coming home at last. I was anxious about how we would be received and how to get a job. We were quite completely broke with only a suitcase full of old clothes.

Our first stop was at the immigration station on Silver Street with all the other foreigners. Here they checked us out to see if we were fit to enter the United States. There were plenty of questions to answer, especially since we had come from the Soviet Union. At one point it was suggested that if the United States did not accept us we would be shipped back to the Soviet Union.

"Never!" I remember saying. "I will never go back. I'll jump off the ship."

It took a couple of months to get things straightened out. On the advice of one of the inspectors, I even wrote a letter to Washington explaining everything as well as I could. The fact that Hitler attacked Russia in June and the Soviet Union became our ally helped us.

Everyone at the immigration center was very nice to us, but after seven years we were really anxious to get out and start living again. It was also difficult to stay there because Sylvi was living on the women's side while I had to stay on the men's, except for a couple hours of visiting every day.

We were able to exercise in one part of the building. There was a ping pong table there that I used a lot with a German fellow and a Mexican whose skill was about even with mine. I also recall playing poker and noticing that some of the cards were marked. I told my Mexican friend about it after the game but he already knew and seemed to think it quite common. He was trying to learn the markings himself, but I thought that was too much trouble and concentrated instead on reading and making string belts.

Meals there were good—they even served desserts. Once when we had finished dinner, there was one piece of pie left, and my Mexican friend suggested that I pretend to be Russia, he would be Germany, and the pie we would call Poland. We divided the territory and thus history repeated itself.

July 28 was the day we were free to go. We called Sylvi's Aunt Anna and Uncle Charlie in Berkeley; they came right out to get us and treated us like long lost kids. Aunt Anna took Sylvi shopping and bought her things. They even took us on a trip to Fort Bragg—a beautiful drive along the Pacific coast. I enjoyed the whole trip very much. The people we visited in Fort Bragg made us welcome. They wined and dined us and kept urging us to eat more. I took them up on it, believe me. Besides a big dinner, I ate a whole smoked lobster by myself.

We spent a couple of weeks with Aunt Anna and Uncle Charlie. I registered for the draft and looked for work at the shipyards but jobs were still pretty scarce, and so we took a bus for Detroit—the last leg of our trip around the world.

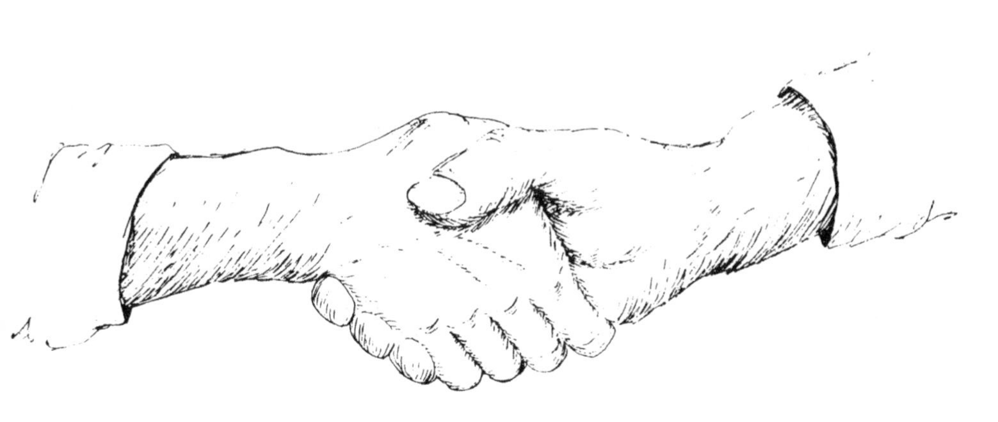

Welcome Home

S: Now we were back in our native land, the United States of America, the land where we'd been born, where we'd spent our childhood and youth, the land of the free. How did we feel? We felt a deep relief, a great happiness that comes at the end of a tortuous journey. Happy and relieved . . . but still worried, not completely relaxed. Questions persisted. How would we be received by our friends? What should we tell them? Would they accept our stories? Would our government allow us to stay since, through our ignorance and thoughtlessness, we had lost our citizenship? These matters were on our minds constantly, although our general feeling was one of deep satisfaction.

We were surprised and pleased at the welcome we received from my Aunt Anna and her family in California. They took us into their home and treated us as long lost members of the family. Throughout their lives Aunt and Uncle had definitely leaned toward the left in their politics, but they showed no resentment toward us for having abandoned the fight for the workingman's cause. They even wanted us to move to California and begin our new life there. But we were eager to get back to Michigan, to Sugar Island, home.

L: We arrived in Detroit after midnight on August 16th, and didn't feel like calling anyone at that hour so we sat in the bus station till morning. After seven years, we felt a bit hesitant to call people, not being sure how we would be received. In the morning we called some old friends named Lehtela who used to spend summers on Sugar Island. They wanted us to come to their place.

Our feet were swollen, we were dirty, the only sleep we'd had in three days was dozing on the bus, so we took hot baths and slept until some time in the afternoon. It felt so good to be clean and rested.

That afternoon Mrs. Lehtela called her daughter Valma. She welcomed us with open arms and then took us to her home. She had a brand new, beautiful house. To us, she and her husband seemed like very rich people. We wondered how they could afford it but did not question them.

Later that day we got in touch with some of our other old friends, including Ingrid and Paul Middleton who said they were planning to go to Sugar Island soon and asked if we would like to go along. That was perfect for us.

For the next few days we visited with old friends and relatives in Detroit getting to know them all over again. They were all so good to us; no one condemned us for having left the State or for coming back. They certainly made us feel that this was where we belonged. I had offers of help in getting employment, and some even offered me jobs, but we wanted to get back to Sugar Island and see my folks before deciding where we would locate.

We rode with Paul and Ingrid through the night and arrived on the island in the morning of August 20th. Everything seemed to be pretty much the same there as when we'd left. My parents' home was in worse shape and needed a new roof, which I proceeded to do as my first job.

There was a welcome-home party for us at my parents house—mostly people whom we had known for a long time. They hadn't aged much—the big change was in the kids, now in their teens. They were so grown up that I had a hard time recognizing them. We were pleased that so many came to our party—more than we had expected. They brought coffee and lunch with them and had a collection for us even though times were still hard, and no one had much money. One man gave me $2.50 that he owed me for sawmill work I had done for him before we left. Another fellow offered me a job running his sawmill for two dollars a day. A friend who was on vacation from his auto repair job down in Detroit told me to come down, and he would get me a job too.

But there was one sour note that afternoon. A fellow from the Soo made a welcoming speech. He said very little about us but got into politics, bragging about the Soviet Union. Among other things, he said that no innocent people had been arrested there. I was about to object to that but could not get a word in at that point, and so I let it go. I have regretted ever since that I did not speak up, but because I knew how my mother felt, I remained silent.

I have already said that my mother was never able to believe the awful things that had happened in Karelia. My sister Irja shared her views, and so it was very hard for us to discuss anything about the Soviet Union with her. She either would not or could not believe us when we tried to tell her our story about what was happening in Karelia and all over the Soviet Union. She would just clam up or get very upset whenever we brought it up. So with her, too, we felt it best to remain silent.

We returned to Detroit where job opportunities seemed better. Sylvi was pregnant, and I did not want her to go to work. I got a job in a gas station right away, and we rented a little room nearby. It wasn't very nice, but it was all we could afford at that time. Paul and Ingrid visited us there and afterwards invited us to come and stay with them, which we did for a few months. After that we stayed with a family named Waisanen for a while.

The life-styles of all our friends impressed us; they seemed so free to indulge in whatever they preferred to do. We were also amazed by their nice new autos and the beautiful homes with modern conveniences. This had all happened in the seven years since we had left Detroit. Their lives had improved dramatically compared to our lives in Karelia. We had worked hard but had nothing to show for it. Somehow it felt as if the revolution had happened here in the United States! Later, our friends told us they had gotten FHA government loans to build their homes. President Roosevelt, they also told us, was the man who had brought this about. He pulled the country out of the Great Depression, which had been one of the factors influencing our decision to go to Russia. It proves what a good president can do.

In February of 1942 I landed a job in a tool and die shop. Our daughter Anita was born two weeks later. The people in the shop were very good to me. They knew I had been in Russia. Only a few were interested enough to ask me how I had liked it. I would say that I didn't and would never go back. Occasionally someone would want to know how much money we made, and I would tell them, also explaining that all our pay went for food and drink.

I had registered with the draft board as soon as we arrived in California, but since I was in defense work at the tool and die company, they got a deferrment for me. I stayed with that company until my retirement in 1971.

We did not talk much about our life in Karelia with anyone over here. Once I remember when I was at our hunting camp with several friends, a fellow I had met after we came back began to ask me why I had gone to Russia and what it was like. Before I even had time to answer, an old friend of mine spoke up and told him he had no right to question me about that. It had taken a lot of guts for me to go there, he said angrily. I didn't like the sound of this argument so I just suggested we have another drink instead. I really wouldn't have minded telling them about it, but that subject always stirred up strong feelings.

S: Our homecoming to Sugar Island was most traumatic for me. My father and brother had died while we were away and I felt their loss keenly on returning to my childhood home where everything reminded me of them. The old farmhouse and hall where my father had spent so much of his time and energy were more than I could bear, and I refused to let our Sugar Island friends hold our welcome home party at the hall. One elderly woman accused me of being afraid to be seen at the hall because it had communist connections, but that was furthest from my thoughts. I was thinking only of my father and brother and my sorrow at their deaths.

My brother Arvo, the only remaining member of my family, was in a tuberculosis sanitarium at this time and would remain there for another year. He had never had the least interest in politics. We could have discussed our experiences with him but never did. Even after he came to live with us, we shied away from the subject, as we did with other people, thinking no one was interested. It was a part of our lives we would do well to forget.

But of course, we couldn't forget. What we had left was much on our minds as we adjusted to our new life in the States. The few friends we'd known in Detroit earlier welcomed us and brought us into a bigger group of their own where we soon became members in good standing. This group was made up primarily of second generation American Finns. Their parents had been active in socialist, and some, perhaps, in communist groups, but, as we have mentioned before, within the second generation Finns, class consciousness had abated. Politically, they were either Democratic or Republican depending on their circumstances. They all knew we had been in the Soviet Union, but no one questioned us because, as we later learned, they felt we were the ones who should bring it up. We, on the other hand, did not want to talk about our experiences since we felt that they did not care to hear about them. This feeling was reinforced by occasional comments such as one I remember during the war. I was with a group of women one evening when many complaints about shortages were brought up: silk stockings were scarce, bakery items were hard to come by, etc. I felt these women were pampered; they did not really know what shortages were! So I tried to tell them. When you stand all night in a queue for a pound of meat or sugar, you don't see coffee for months on end, you don't even dream of silk stockings or bakery cakes—these, to me, were shortages. One of the ladies glared at me and said, "I'm sure you didn't starve over there."

I had not intended, and could not have conveyed, any such idea. I just wanted them to know how lucky they were, and how childish their complaints seemed. But after that, I never tried to tell them of what we went through.

Occasionally, we had some contact with people connected in some way to our life in Russia. In 1941, Keijo's mother, Mrs. Frilund, came to see us. This was the first time we'd met her. She was very kind and understanding and listened to all the news we had of her son and his family. Although this was bad news—her son had been arrested, and his family evicted from their home—she did not seem to hold it against the Soviet government. It seemed, rather, that she felt these things could happen but that in time all would be corrected. Although the world was by then embroiled in World War II, she exclaimed that it was such an interesting time to be living. She evidently had a larger than ordinary view of world events, and saw everything as history in the making. The future held her interest and in connection with this, children. Children were all important to her. When we saw her again in 1946, we noticed many instances when she preferred to hear what our four-year-old Anita wanted to say than to listen to us. We do not know whether she had wished to emigrate to the Soviet Union with her son and family but if she had, and had been rejected, it could very well have because she was the kind of person whom the party in the States did not want to lose.

In 1945 we were able to get in touch with Urho and Irma Hill who were living in Sault Ste. Marie, Canada. We saw much of them over the years. Urho, having held onto his Canadian passport, was able to return to his homeland in the spring of 1938. Irma had to wait for permission to join him which did not come until the fall of that year. During the big purge at the ski factory that summer she, too, had been evicted from her room along with all those women whose men had been arrested. Because she had a small baby, she was not sent to Lime Island with the others but to a kolkhoz near Petrozavodsk where she remained until allowed to leave the country.

Urho's father had been arrested during the summer of 1938 and was never heard from again. His mother, after much suffering during the war, managed to get to the American Embassy in Moscow where she served as a cook for some time. The Embassy was instrumental in getting her back to Canada. It was war time, so they put her on an Army plane going to England. From there she eventually made her way home to Sault Ste. Marie, Ontario. Both she and Urho have since died, but Irma still lives in the Soo and we meet occasionally.

Aside from Urho and Irma we had no one with whom we could talk freely of our common experience. It was a relief to discuss these events, and I found it sad that we could not talk about them with others because they wouldn't have or couldn't have understood.

After Anita entered school, I became involved with the Girl Scouts and later on with the United Way organization (then called the Red Feather). I made many new friends among the other mothers but to none of them did I confide the fact that we had lived in the Soviet Union. These women were not involved in leftist politics; in fact, as far as I could tell, they were not interested in any kind of politics. They could not have known anything about Karelia or the issues that took us there or caused our return. I am still in contact with one friend from this period, and she does not to this day know of our life in Russia.

It took many years before we were able to regain our United States citizenship. We were technically "aliens" at that time and had to register at the post office every year. We were not supposed to travel to foreign countries, so we never visited our friends in Canada or even went to Boblo Island, a Canadian-owned amusement park in the Detroit River.

Our first application for citizenship was turned down. We don't know why. We had to have sponsors to speak in our behalf and had chosen an elderly Finnish couple whose English was not very good. We have since wondered whether they answered correctly all the questions put to them about us. They themselves were not sure that they had. Possibly, though, we were turned down simply because this was the McCarthy era when Senator Joe McCarthy of Wisconsin was leading a national witch hunt for communists in government and other influential positions. Lauri and I were called in for questioning by the Federal Bureau of Investigation once during that time. I remember that the inspector asked me if we had ever belonged to the communist party, and I said, "no." Then he asked me why I had gone to the Soviet Union. I told him I had gone because my husband went. "That's a very good answer," he told me. Lauri, who was questioned separately, was asked about several friends and acquaintances: were they communists? He said he didn't know, and we were never called in for questioning again.

We made our second application for citizenship as soon as we were allowed to do so. We took our good friend Paul Middleton and another Finnish-American who owned his own business as sponsors. This time we were granted full citizenship. It was a red letter day for us—September 29, 1953—one of the most important and happiest of our lives. We had regained our birthright. We were home at last.

We remained in Detroit for thirty years. When Lauri, whom we now call Lawrence, retired in 1971 we moved back to Sugar Island and have lived there year round ever since, with occasional trips to other parts of the United States. Twice during these years we have visited friends and relatives in Finland. Although Finland is next door to Karelia, we have not as yet ventured there due to the fact that upon our departure back in 1941 we had to sign a paper promising never to return. The reason for this has never been clear to us.

We have had a good happy life with much to be thankful for. After our return Paul Middleton and his wife, Ingrid, became our closest family friends. In 1960 our daughter Anita married their son Len. It has been a wonderful relationship all around. We lost Paul in 1981 and Ingrid this past year. We miss them very much. Lawrence and I are growing quite old, but we still get around and are enjoying our "golden years."

Having seen what can happen in a country ruled by the "Dictatorship of the Proletariat" we have become keenly aware of the personal freedom enjoyed here in the United States. In Karelia, the government decided where we could live and work—here it is a personal matter. In the Soviet Union the government kept track of its citizens by issuing passports which had to be shown to the proper authorities wherever one moved. Here a passport is needed only when leaving the country. Elections in the Soviet Union were simple: candidates were chosen from above; voters had only to approve. Here we have a real choice which often requires deliberating on the pros and cons of each candidate. People who have constantly been told what to do can find decision making difficult!

Although when we left for Karelia, we had no clear concept of what either "democracy" or "dictatorship of the proletariat" meant, by degrees we found out. Having become thoroughly disillusioned by the latter, we feel that democracy is the way to go.

We have written and talked much about the wrongs suffered by the people who were recruited to the Soviet Union from Canada and the United States. We remember the terrible things done to our friends and relatives who were innocent of any wrong doing. The Stalinist purges left their mark on all of us. We were left with a feeling of fear and hatred toward those who had committed these wrongs. A few of us escaped. We were lucky to be allowed to return to our native land to a life of ease compared to what we'd been through. I personally left with a feeling of guilt that we had somehow let our friends down. Why were we spared? We do not know to this day. Why were our friends forced to remain to face more hardships and sufferings? It was all terribly unfair. We were left with a deep feeling of sorrow and disappointment that the dream we'd had—the dream we'd worked hard to fulfill—had collapsed around us. We had been sure that, although we faced primitive conditions at first, it would all change and that our work would bring rewards in the way of a better life. At first it did. Our lives were improving. But then came 1937 and 1938. The purges. Arrests and disappearances. Prisons and labor camps. The end for thousands of fellow workers. We can never forget.

L: All in all, our life since we came back to the United States has been a happy one. We are able to say what we think without any qualms about someone being able to harm us for our beliefs. They can refute or criticize what we say, but they cannot put us in jail for saying it.

We are very interested in what is happening in the Soviet Union today and read everything we can find about it. We have a soft spot in our hearts for the Russian people and are happy to hear that they have found some freedom, which they did not have while we were there.

It is good, too, that all the horrors of the purges have come out and are common knowledge, in the Soviet Union as well as here in the United States. I have been able to go to some of those people who didn't believe me back in 1941 when I tried to tell them about events in Karelia and say, "Do you remember what I told you years ago? I knew you didn't believe me then, but now you know that I was not lying." I am glad they know that now, and we just have to forgive them for not believing us in the first place.

This openness, this *glasnost*, in the Soviet Union is a good thing but isn't there more that should be done? We have not heard of any compensation for the widows and children of those innocent people who were arrested during the purges and died in labor camps. We have not heard of any court trials of those who ordered these arrests or those who ran these slave labor camps. All that the families of purge victims have received is a document clearing their relative, posthumously, of the crimes charged. Some of those who were responsible for their deaths are still living in luxury in their townhouses and dachas. Let them stand trial in open court for their crimes. Then, after justice is done, we can go on living in friendship and harmony.

Epilogue

S: For many years after we returned to the United States we had no contact with the friends we'd left in Karelia. The war between Germany and the Soviet Union began, and the Finns in Petrozavodsk were evacuated and sent to faraway places. Those who survived the war slowly found their way back to their former homes after peace was declared. In the years since then we have heard from a few.

In 1957, the year Sputnik went up, we received a surprise letter from our seamstress friend, Edla. She wrote sending "greetings from this land of miracles" and added ingenuously that the Soviet government had instructed its citizens to send such messages to anyone they knew in other countries. From then on we corresponded sporadically with her. Her son Vilho had been in the Red Army during World War II and had been taken prisoner by the Finns. When he was returned to the Soviet Union in a prisoner exchange after the war, he was imprisoned there for having allowed himself to be taken by the enemy. This was common; a Red Army soldier does not give himself up to the enemy! During his eight years in a Soviet prison, he contracted tuberculosis. He'd been sentenced for ten years but came home when Kruschev came into power and allowed many prisoners to be freed.

In the sixties, Edla, Vilho and Vilho's wife, Evi moved to Estonia where Edla died some years later. Vilho and Evi are still there and we correspond; our letters deal mostly with events and observations having to do with our day to day lives. We hesitate to discuss politics for fear of causing them trouble.

Richie, who lived across the hallway in our barrack on Swamp Street, died in the war. His older sister Lilian has been writing to us for some years. After returning to Petrozavodsk when the war ended, she taught school and lived with her mother who died a few years ago. In her letters, Lilian has written of many amusing incidents involving us which her mother recalled. Now retired, Lilian lives quietly and seems generally satisfied with her life.

Dave and Lily's daughter, Viola, is also in Petrozavodsk. In the early seventies, she wrote that her father was still alive in Rovaniemi, Finland. In 1972 we made a trip to Finland and looked him up. We found him living with a Lapp woman who was proud of receiving visitors from America; she hoped all the neighbors had taken note of our arrival. Dave's trip across the border in 1938 with Vilho and Terttu had been hazardous and difficult—traveling mostly by night, sleeping in the woods, ever on the alert for border guards who had the authority to shoot on sight anyone who was crossing the border without a permit.

In 1977 Viola was able to make a trip to the States. Relatives here helped with technicalities such as the invitation needed by Russians in order to visit a foreign country and also assurance that these same relatives would be responsible in case of her illness or other emergencies. Viola told us that Lily had died of cancer a few years earlier. Her brother Hugo had disappeared during the war. Viola was amazed at all she saw here: the abundance of food and goods available, the cars—in many cases several in a family—the freedom with which we moved about wherever we pleased with no need to report to authorities. Since all of us had so much more than we needed, we sent her back loaded with gifts of all sorts.

Flossie, my schoolmate from the Pedagogical Institute, learned of my whereabouts several years ago, and we have exchanged a few letters. She too found her way back to Petrozavodsk after the war, married and raised a family. She is now a retired school teacher and lives with her husband, their children having grown up and married. Back in 1938, when we had decided to apply for permission to leave the Soviet Union, Flossie accompanied me to Moscow to the American Embassy to start the process. While we were there she was asked by one of the officials if she also wanted to leave the country. "I will never leave here," she replied. Her belief in the future of the Soviet Union has always appeared firm. Only recently did she wonder why her parents had gone there.

Our little Heikki had died of malnutrition while still quite young. His father, Viljo, and mother, Tyyne, died in nursing homes a few years ago. Viljo had been sent to Finland as a spy during World War II and had been caught. Upon being returned to the Soviet Union after the war, he was imprisoned there for several years. When we knew Tyyne she was a happy-go-lucky, fun loving person but, as we later learned, her wartime experiences left her very embittered.

On a more recent visit to Finland we met with Aune and Tauno Salo, another couple from our Petrozavodsk days, some of the last we'd seen there before we left. For them, too, the war had been a period of sickness and near starvation. Then after Stalin's death and Kruschev's rise to power, there was a period when it was possible for them to move to Finland to be with his elderly parents. They took advantage of this and are now living comfortably. While with them we spent many hours reminiscing and learned the fate of many of our friends.

Benny Laine's wife Miriam is still living in Karelia. So also is Inki Kent. Her husband, Walter, had perished in the war. On our last trip to Finland, we met Inki's daughter and granddaughter. My schoolmate Inkeri Letonmaki, we learned, died quite recently. The Salos also told us that the young man who had been arrested for borrowing the Sinclair Lewis book was never released.

We have never heard what happened to my Uncle Frank and his family. His daughter, who is still living here in the states, has not been able to get any information as to their fate.

My former classmate Selma Anderson, her mother, sister and son were the only others we know of who were given permission to leave at the time we were. They followed us during the summer of 1941, also by way of Japan. Selma's father and husband had died in Karelia. They had been recruited in 1931 to work in the iron mines in Siberia. By 1934, they were in Petrozavodsk where Selma attended the Pedagogical Institute and was one of our small group who met to study together. She lives now in New York; during all these years we have visited her only once, but we correspond. She has told us of the many troubles and worries she had while in Petrozavodsk and during the time she made arrangements for her return to the States.

Martha Nieminen (the sister of our good friend Paul Middleton) is still living in Leningrad. Her husband Dave and daughter Ella both died during the war. Now ninety-two years old, Martha travels a lot in the Soviet Union and makes frequent trips to Finland where she has many friends and relatives. In 1981, she made a trip to the United States. Her sister in Florida offered to take care of her if she would stay and live with her, but Martha chose to return to the Soviet Union where she had lived for fifty years and had many friends. On our last trip to Finland we met Martha and found her to be still healthy in body and mind with a great interest in world events.

Our good friends Sylvi and Eino Dahlstrom died years ago, he of tuberculosis contracted at a labor camp. Sylvi and her mother had been among the evacuees sent across the Urals for the duration of the war. After returning to Petrozavodsk, Sylvi died of heart trouble.

L: I heard that during World War II Eino had been detained at some camp for foreigners in the Soviet Union. Some NKVD big shots had stopped at the camp one day and then weren't able to get their car started when it was time to leave. When they asked if someone at the camp could start it for them, Eino had volunteered to look it over. Being a good auto mechanic (one of the best) he had it going in no time. The big shots were so impressed that they said he was in the wrong place, and let him out so he was able to go to work, thereby getting more food and better accommodations. I was glad to hear that, but I guess Eino didn't live much longer after that. I sure wish our friends could have left the Soviet Union when we did.

S: With the sister-city movement building up between the United States and the Soviet Union, we are experiencing more contact with our Russian friends. As a coincidence, the city of Petrozavodsk, where we lived, and Duluth, the American city that is home to our daughter and her family, are sister cities. Because of this relationship, we have met some people from our old home town. Furthermore, our son-in-law, Len Middleton, was able to make a trip to Petrozavodsk with one of the sister-city groups. He met several of our old friends who still live there and brought back pictures of them, along with a picture of the old barrack we used to live in: barrack 50 on Swamp Street (the street has a different name now). What memories it brought back. At present Len is urging us to make a trip with him and Anita next year, to see for ourselves what changes have been wrought since we were there. We hesitate. . . .

Bibliography

Dallin, David J. *The Real Soviet Russia*. Trans. by Joseph Shaplen. Yale University Press, 1944.

Hosking, Geoffrey. *The First Socialist Society*. Harvard University Press, 1985.

Kivisto, Peter. *Immigrant Socialists in the United States; the case of the Finns and the Left*. Associated University Presses, 1984.

Kort, Michael. *The Soviet Colossus; A History of the U.S.S.R.* Charles Scribner's Sons, New York, 1985.

Randall, Francis B. *Stalin's Russia; An Historical Reconsideration*. The Free Press, New York, 1965.

Rostow, W.W. *The Dynamics of Soviet Society*. Massachusetts Institute of Technology, 1954.

Timasheff, Nicholas S. *The Great Retreat; The Growth and Decline of Communism in Russia*. Dutton, New York, 1946.

Tuominen, Arvo. *The Bells of the Kremlin; an experience in communism*. Piltti Heiskanen, Editor. Lily Leino, translator. University Press of New England, Hanover and London, 1983.

Made in the USA
Monee, IL
21 March 2022